STUDIES IN ECONOMIC HISTORY

This series, specially commissioned by the Economic History Society, focuses attention on the main problems of economic history. Recently there has been a great deal of detailed research and reinterpretation, some of it controversial, but it has remained largely inaccessible to students or buried in academic journals. This series is an attempt to provide a guide to the current interpretations of the key themes of economic history in which advances have recently been made, or in which there has been significant debate.

Each book will survey recent work, indicate the full scope of the particular problem as it has been opened by research and distinguish what conclusions can be drawn in the present state of knowledge. Both old and recent work will be reviewed critically, but each book will provide a balanced survey rather than an exposition of the author's own viewpoint.

The series as a whole will give readers access to the best work done, help them to draw their own conclusions in some major fields and, by means of the critical bibliography in each book, guide them in the selection of further reading. The aim is to provide a springboard to further work and not a set of prepackaged conclusions or short cuts.

STUDIES IN ECONOMIC HISTORY

Edited for the Economic History Society by
M. W. Flinn

PUBLISHED

TITLES IN PREPARATION INCLUDE

Depression and Recovery?

British Economic Growth, 1918–1939

Prepared for
The Economic History Society by

B. W. E. ALFORD

Lecturer in Economic History
in the University of Bristol

MACMILLAN

First published 1972 by
THE MACMILLAN PRESS LTD
London and Basingstoke

*Associated companies in New York Toronto
Dublin Melbourne Johannesburg and Madras*

SBN 333 11235 0

Printed in Great Britain by
THE ANCHOR PRESS LTD
Tiptree, Essex

Contents

List of Tables

Acknowledgements

I am grateful to Professor William Ashworth and Professor M. W. Flinn, who read the manuscript and made valuable suggestions. I should also like to thank Mr David Large for his advice on certain aspects of the political history of the period.

The photographs on the cover of the Jarrow march, 1936, and of an Austin motor-car assembly line in the 1930s are reproduced by permission, respectively, of the Radio Times Hulton Picture Library, and of British Leyland (Austin-Morris) Ltd.

Bristol   B. W. E. A.
1971

Editor's Preface

SO long as the study of economic history was confined to only a small group at a few universities, its literature was not prolific and its few specialists had no great problem in keeping abreast of the work of their colleagues. Even in the 1930s there were only two journals devoted exclusively to this field. But the high quality of the work of the economic historians during the inter-war period and the post-war growth in the study of the social sciences sparked off an immense expansion in the study of economic history after the Second World War. There was a great expansion of research and many new journals were launched, some specialising in branches of the subject like transport, business or agricultural history. Most significantly, economic history began to be studied as an aspect of history in its own right in schools. As a consequence, the examining boards began to offer papers in economic history at all levels, while textbooks specifically designed for the school market began to be published.

For those engaged in research and writing this period of rapid expansion of economic history studies has been an exciting, if rather breathless one. For the larger numbers, however, labouring in the outfield of the schools and colleges of further education, the excitement of the explosion of research has been tempered by frustration caused by its vast quantity and, frequently, its controversial character. Nor, it must be admitted, has the ability or willingness of the academic economic historians to generalise and summarise marched in step with their enthusiasm for research.

The greatest problems of interpretation and generalisation have tended to gather round a handful of principal themes in economic history. It is, indeed, a tribute to the sound sense of economic historians that they have continued to dedicate their energies, however inconclusively, to the solution of these key problems. The results of this activity, however, much of it stored away in a wide range of academic journals, have tended to remain inaccessible to many of those currently interested in the subject. Recognising the need for guidance through the burgeoning and confusing literature that has grown around these basic topics, the Economic History Society decided to launch this series of small books. The books are intended to serve as guides to current interpretations in important fields of economic history in which important advances have recently been made, or in which there has recently been some significant debate. Each book aims to survey recent work, to indicate the full scope of the particular problem as it has been opened up by recent scholarship, and to draw such conclusions as seem warranted, given the present state of knowledge and understanding. The authors will often be at pains to point out where, in their view, because of a lack of information or inadequate research, they believe it is premature to attempt to draw firm conclusions. While authors will not hesitate to review recent and older work critically, the books are not intended to serve as vehicles for their own specialist views: the aim is to provide a balanced summary rather than an exposition of the author's own viewpoint. Each book will include a descriptive bibliography.

In this way the series aims to give all those interested in economic history at a serious level access to recent scholarship in some major fields. Above all, the aim is to help the reader to draw his own conclusions, and to guide him in the selection of further reading as a means to this end, rather than to present him with a set of pre-packaged conclusions.

M. W. FLINN
Editor

Bibliographical Note

REFERENCES in the text for which full details are given in the Select Bibliography simply quote the author's name, date of publication referred to and page number(s) where appropriate, e.g. Grant (1937, 100).

1 The Problem

IN recent years the economic performance of Britain in the inter-war period has proved an attractive subject among economic historians. It is, of course, a particularly convenient period for historical analysis : it begins with the effects of one world war and ends with preparations for a second, even more disastrous, one. And from the viewpoint of social and economic history the most dramatic feature of the period is the persistently high level of unemployment. Indeed, what might be called the traditional view is that these years were overcast with economic depression which brought severe hardship to large sections of the community. This characterisation has its origins in the literature of the period itself. There is, for example, the bleak picture painted by Orwell's *The Road to Wigan Pier* (1937) and the social decay and disillusion portrayed in Greenwood's novel, *Love on the Dole* (1933). Moreover, such events as the General Strike and the 'hunger marches' bear testimony to the degree of social and political tension which existed.

A closer look at the evidence, however, reveals that the picture is by no means entirely a study in black – that it is one of contrasts. This is perhaps best illustrated by Priestley in his *English Journey* (1934), in which he distinguishes four Englands : there was the nineteenth-century England of the industrial North; there was the 'England of the Dole' whose boundaries were very close to those of nineteenth-century England – though 'if one's view took in the whole of Great Britain, it would include all industrial Scotland, all South Wales, and most of North Wales as well'. But standing against these Englands were two others : the 'old England of the southern counties and the guide books'; and 'twentieth-century England . . . the England of the bustling home counties, of by-passes and housing estates and suburban

13

villas and cocktail bars gleaming with chromium trim' (cited in Mowat, 1955, 480–90). After all, these years also saw the widespread introduction of a whole new range of consumer goods and services, including motor-cars, electric cookers, radios, rayon underwear and talkie films. And although many might have regretted the dawning of this brash new world, it did bring with it improvement in living standards for some sections of the community.

For many years economic historians have been well aware of this brighter side to the period, but recently the availability of more detailed statistical data has encouraged some economic historians to attempt to place the economic performance of the inter-war years into clearer perspective. This has led to some of them suggesting that the period as a whole was one of significant economic progress, and that as such it compares favourably with the half-century or so before 1914. This form of revisionism has almost developed into a new orthodoxy, and it is perhaps as well, therefore, to begin our review by a consideration of this interpretation and the statistical data on which it is based.

2 The Growth Record

BEFORE we examine the data in detail, it is first of all important to distinguish between the cyclical features of the economy
and its longer-term growth performance. Economic theorists have
for long wrestled with the complex problem of relating these two
aspects to one another, and in historical terms the problem is
probably insoluble. As Svennilson has pointed out (1954, 12–13)
in his study of the European economy in the inter-war period, the
economic historian can indicate the relationships between the two
aspects of economic change but cannot integrate them into a
general explanation.

There were fairly well-defined fluctuations, or cycles, in the
level of economic activity during this period. Immediately after
the war there was a boom which collapsed into a severe slump in
1921–2. This was followed by a weak and uneven upswing which
reached its high point in 1929, though in certain respects – particularly in the export sector – the level of economic performance
remained below pre-war level. The depression of the early thirties
is well known, with its trough being reached in 1932. This was
followed by a revival, which lasted until 1937, when there was a
further sharp downswing. Finally, just before the Second World
War, the economy picked up strongly once more. A detailed
analysis of these swings shows, however, that there was far from
being a single set of causal factors. Britain's weak export performance undoubtedly operated as a general constraint, particularly
at the upper turning-points, but there was a variety of other
short-term factors which distinguished one cycle from another.
For example, there are the contrasts between the war-induced
boom of 1919–20, the revival based on the growth of new consumer goods and building in the early thirties, and the rearmament boom at the end of the period. The nature of these

15

short-term influences will become clearer in subsequent discussion

Yet although the causes of cycles in economic activity varied, they occurred around and in relation to a long-term trend in economic growth, and this trend provides the real measure of the economy's performance over time. And it is on this aspect that the debate over the achievement of the British economy between the wars has been centred.

The most important statistical series that have been produced, over the last decade or so, relate to national income and expenditure, domestic and foreign investment, and production and productivity. Moreover, mainly on the basis of the last series, estimates of gross domestic product have been constructed, and it is these figures which have been mostly used as the measure for evaluating the overall performance of the economy. Even before the recent crop of estimates became available, however, revisionism was first preached by Richardson (1961) in an article which laid stress on the importance of the 'new' industries between the wars. Some years earlier Sayers (1950) had drawn attention to the wide range of new techniques which became available between the wars, and Richardson sought to put some flesh on these bones by collecting together evidence of the expansion of industrial production based on these techniques. The balance of evidence thus produced pointed to the 1930s, as against the 1920s, as being the period of particularly rapid change.

This approach to the economic development of the inter-war period has gradually been elaborated into a thesis of 'economic recovery' in the 1930s. Basically, the argument is that after the sharp depression of the early thirties, the British economy showed noticeable vigour over the remainder of the decade, or at least up to the recession of 1937–8. This 'recovery' was based on a conjunction of supply and demand factors. So far as the former were concerned, these years saw the eventual coming to fruition of a number of innovations in what are described as 'new' industries. These were predominantly consumer-goods industries and included such things as motor-vehicles, electrical goods and artificial fibres, which in effect formed a development block in the economy, not least through their connection with the building boom of the mid-thirties. On the demand side, the price-falls and

16

higher unemployment recorded during the depression resulted in a redistribution of income from the unemployed to the employed, especially in favour of the lower and middle income groups. Taken together, these factors generated expansion. Considerable emphasis is laid on the sectoral nature of these changes, since on both the supply and demand sides aggregate indicators – such as the total level of consumption – do not show marked increases. But, it is argued, the important changes are discernible at the disaggregate level. In other words, the thesis attempts to combine cyclical behaviour with structural change; though it argues that this provides no support for the autonomous theory of the trade cycle, since the conjunction of rising real income and technical innovation was, in a general sense, fortuitous. And finally, so far as two other well-known features of the period were concerned – 'cheap money' and the building boom – the former was a permissive and not a causal factor, whereas the latter was important but by no means decisive.

To complete the argument, it is of course necessary to answer the question of why it was not until the 1930s that the breakthrough occurred. And the answer is given in terms of 'overcommitment' in the British economy; this was a cumulative process which occurred largely during the years before 1914 and involved the piling up of resources in sectors of the economy which did not possess the potential for high long-term growth but which, nevertheless, accounted for such a large proportion of the economy's resources as to constitute a log-jam in factor redistribution; over-commitment retarded growth by making factors scarce for new industries, by debilitating entrepreneurial effort, and by distorting the institutional framework (in particular the capital market), in a manner which made 'the adoption of new industries . . . less economic in Britain than abroad' (Richardson, 1965, 242). With the added gloss of more comprehensive statistics and with some minor modifications in analysis, Richardson (1967) combined these arguments into a lengthy and comprehensive treatise on economic recovery in Britain between 1932 and 1939.

Once under way, the revisionist school has quickly gained new adherents, and among the first was Lomax (1964) who offered

17

an interpretation of his production index, which had first appeared in 1959.[1] This index shows that over the period 1920–37 industrial growth was occurring at the rate of 3·1 per cent per annum; while for the sub-periods 1920–9 and 1929–37 the corresponding rates are 2·8 per cent and 3·3 per cent per annum. In the light of this, for Lomax, the period is one of substantial growth, and the reasons he gives for it are, again, a combination of supply and demand factors : during the 1920s new industries were expanding as the result of innovation and upward shifts in demand for their products brought about by the income effects of the favourable movement in the terms of trade (see below, Section 5, pp. 57–64). As part and parcel of this process there was a switch in the balance of investment, as compared with the pre-war period, from the foreign to the domestic sector which was higher in 'real terms' than appears from the available data because of falling prices of capital goods in the latter period. And lastly, while the effects of government policy are not altogether clear, at least for the 1930s Lomax considers it possible to isolate certain 'stimulating measures' taken by the Government : devaluation; the introduction of tariffs; cheap money; direct help to industry.

Contemporaneous with Lomax's interpretation of his own data, Feinstein (1963) and Matthews (1964) produced general estimates of gross domestic product and its main constituents. Matthews offered, also, some rough calculations on the sources of growth, in terms of factor inputs, for 1856 to 1962, and, in particular, for the sub-periods 1924–37 and 1948–62. Both studies lend support to the view that the inter-war period saw a return to the longer-term growth rates of the latter half of the nineteenth century which, for various reasons, had not been equalled over the period 1900–24. Matthews goes a little further than this, however, by indicating that he favours the interpretation which lays stress on the 1930s as the dominant period of growth between 1918 and 1939.

[1] Industrial production includes manufacturing industry; mining and quarrying; building and contracting; gas, water and electricity supply.

18

Finally, in some ways the most far-reaching claims for the inter-war period have been advanced by Aldcroft (1966, 1967). In contrast to his view of the quarter century or so before the war as a period of atrophying enterprise, he sees the inter-war years, and particularly the 1920s, as years of rejuvenation of entrepreneurial flair which led to the successful establishment of 'new' industries. The demise of the old staples is seen as having brought businessmen face to face with economic reality which in turn gave a new sense of urgency and action to the process of innovation. Moreover, by drawing on a bewilderingly wide collection of statistical sources, Aldcroft illustrates his argument with comparisons which reflect favourably on the inter-war period when seen against the economic achievement of the other major economies during those years, and against Britain's own performance between 1870 and 1914.

Thus, the case for revising what we have termed the traditional view of the inter-war period, as one of depression and generally poor economic achievement, has been most plausibly advanced. Indeed, it has been suggested that 'it would be profitable if scholars in future devoted more attention to the factors underlying this growth pattern, rather than in discussing the economic disasters which characterised the period' (Aldcroft, 1967, 325). But before this advice is heeded, it is necessary to ask in what sense the inter-war years have been established as a period of economic growth, and also whether other scholars' preoccupation with economic disaster has been determined by a natural proclivity for the macabre, or by the earlier unavailability of comprehensive statistical data, or by mistaken analysis, or, indeed, by any combination of these factors.

The most comprehensive critical appraisal of the arguments which have been outlined has been made by Dowie (1968). By careful analysis of the available data he has placed the economic growth of the period into a clearer and somewhat different perspective. But first of all he underlines the point made by Matthews: that in order to achieve the best possible reliability, calculations of the growth *trend* for the inter-war period have to be based on the benchmark years of 1924 and 1937, with an intermediate date of 1929. On this basis gross domestic product grew at a rate of 2·3 per cent per annum, industrial production excluding building at 3·0 per cent per annum, and output of manufacturing industries, alone, by 3·3 per cent per annum. These rates differ from those used by Lomax and Aldcroft since they have chosen a variety of base years and sub-periods which distort the long-term trend. Lomax and Aldcroft also base their analyses far too much on the one sector of manufacturing industry. Moreover, Dowie, again following Matthews, demonstrates how misleading it is to consider the whole span of time from 1870 to 1914 without drawing attention to the significant break in trends between 1899 and 1913. For example, Aldcroft (1967, 317) quotes the rate of growth of gross domestic product for the period 1899–1913 at 1·1 per cent per annum, as against 2·3 per cent per annum for the years 1924–37; whereas Matthews's figures (1964, Table I) are: 1856–99, 2·0 per cent; 1899–1913, 1·1 per cent.

Having established the point concerning general growth rates, it is then possible for Dowie to consider the 'expansion thesis' in more detail. The figures show that overall growth in gross domestic product in the 1920s and 1930s was broadly similar. There are, however, sectoral differences between the two decades. In general terms, growth over the thirties was maintained by an acceleration in growth in the manufacturing and distribution sectors which offset decelerations elsewhere. But at the same time this switch must not be allowed to obscure the fact that these were *relative* changes within the total: agriculture, for example, failed to maintain its high growth rate of the twenties; and distribution and manufacturing, although improving their performances, were by no means the leading sectors overall.

Labour productivity (measured by output per man-year of employment) certainly rose faster in the 1930s than in the 1920s – 50 per cent faster in fact – but, once again, there was considerable variation between industries. Moreover, this variation cannot be ordered in terms of 'new' and 'old' industries. If, for a moment, it is accepted that 'new' industries can be differentiated, and include chemicals, electrical engineering, vehicles, artificial fibres, precision instruments, paper and printing, and utilities, then these by no means head the ranking of productivity gains; and although, in the 1930s, these industries are to be found among those of most rapid growth in productivity, they are accompanied by others such as textiles and agriculture. Furthermore, the so-called new industries account for rather less than half the labour force employed in the broad group which showed marked acceleration in productivity over the 1930s. For the whole period 1924–37, the 'new' industries appear even less impressive: on a simple ranking chemicals come thirteenth, paper and printing sixteenth, and electrical engineering seventeenth, out of nineteen altogether. And if some attempt were made to weight the industries according to their importance in terms of the value of net output, the so-called 'old' industries would predominate.

Even on a broad basis the distinction between 'old' and 'new' industries does not appear to be a particularly useful one. In a number of cases 'new' industries grew out of 'old' industries and were, in effect, the tangible results of efforts at modernisation; one of the best examples of this is provided by the silk and rayon industry. Moreover, as will be suggested later, this artificial distinction results in large part from defining industries simply in terms of technical innovation, and ignoring such aspects as organisation and management. There is too, as Dowie points out, the danger of defining 'new' in terms of 'expanding', and by this means establishing what it is wished to prove by tautological definition. For the 'new' industry argument to carry conviction, it is necessary to show that such industries form a distinct group; that the majority, if not all, of those so defined were expanding; and that in total this expansion was powerful enough to provide a thrust to economic revival in the early thirties. Considerable doubt has been cast by Dowie on the possibility of the first two criteria being met, and it will be argued that the evidence in support of the third is far from convincing.

Before this aspect is considered in more detail, however, it is necessary to look a little more closely at the available statistical data. For while Dowie's criticisms of the Richardson–Lomax–Aldcroft approach to the inter-war years amounts to a convincing argument for careful use of this kind of evidence, it seems likely

21

that even Dowie does not go far enough in exposing the weaknesses of interpretations based on the various series taken at their face value. Central to most of the calculations of various economic indicators is the Lomax (1959) production index. Now it must be said at once that it is a far easier pastime to criticise an index of this kind than it is to construct one. And it should go without saying that a series such as the Lomax index is of immense value to economists and economic historians. The point of the following observations is that it is important to understand the problems associated with the construction of such an index *before* employing it as a tool of historical explanation. More immediately, one should question whether there are any major stumbling-blocks to using the index for making comparisons over such a short period as 1924–37, even though for statistical reasons it is the only meaningful period which could be chosen during the inter-war years.

Present space does not admit of a full discussion of the methods employed in constructing the index, but these can easily be consulted in the original. It is possible, therefore, to make only a few brief observations, though it is hoped that these will be sufficiently explicit for our purposes. The first point concerns the system of weighting which is based on net value output figures derived from the 1924, 1930 and 1935 censuses of production.[2] There is always the problem of how well net values of certain base years reflect the longer-term position of an industry in total industrial output, but this problem would appear to be unusually acute during the period under review. Because of heavy unemployment and the international depression of primary product prices, which together operated to reduce the cost of inputs and the value of gross outputs of the major staple industries, net value outputs tend to fall off quite sharply over the period between 1924 and

[2] For details on the weighting methods used, see Lomax (1959, 186–91). Net output is the equivalent of the value of work done and goods made *less* the cost of materials used and the amount paid for sub-contract work. It is, therefore, the measure of an industry's 'real' contribution to total production. From this it should be clear why net output figures provide the basis for weighting industries against one another.

the early 1930s, before recovering somewhat towards the very end of the period. Against this, however, volumes of production did not exhibit such marked downswings. Rather, the pattern was one of slump and stagnation punctuated by a few particularly bad years, with some recovery towards the end of the period, which was of more than marginal significance only in the case of iron and steel.[3] So far as the chief staple industries are concerned, the effect of this relationship between value and volume figures is bound to be that in real comparative terms they are under-weighted in the final index; which in turn means that the overall reducing effect of their stagnation on the index is underweighted.

Maizels has drawn attention to another aspect of this problem by arguing that 1930, in particular, is a poor year to take as a base, since it is one in which prices, generally, fell sharply and in which there was a reduction both in physical output and in new orders. 'These changes affecting different industries and products in different ways, almost certainly resulted in an abnormal rela-tionship of the recorded unit values [gross prices] of the main items of output.'[4] Correspondingly, therefore, net output values were distorted and in turn this distorts the weighting employed in the index. More broadly, in addition to the effects of the depression, certain 'new' goods, such as vehicles and electrical equipment, were experiencing a longer-term decline in prices either through substantial gains from economies of scale or through greater concentration on different-quality goods (such as the switch to lower horse-power cars), or through a combina-tion of these factors; and in these cases large price reductions were made *after* 1930. In short, the net result of this is a tendency to overweight the importance of the so-called 'new' industries in 1930.

Another major problem has been indicated by Maizels, namely, that of duplication. The main reason for this would seem to be the existence, in certain industries, of a considerable number of small firms doing contract work for large firms. The Census authorities were well aware of this problem, but the instructions

[3] See chaps. iv, v, vii and xvi in Mitchell and Deane (1962).
[4] See Lomax (1959, 214, discussion section).

they issued in an attempt to avoid double counting seem to have been ignored by many large firms, which did not reduce their net output figures by the amounts they had paid out to smaller firms. The result was that output was frequently counted twice in the Census. The overall effect of this is a distortion of upswings and downswings in activity, since these are usually characterised by the appearance and disappearance of small firms. Typical is the building industry. For example, the Lomax index shows output of building to have risen from 1924=100 to 1930=131, whereas the 1930 Census's own index shows a rise of from 100 to 129. Maizels (1963) suggests that, when allowance is made for 'the increase in total employment and . . . for some increase in productivity it still looks doubtful whether the volume of [building] production increased by more than 20 per cent, after eliminating the duplication in the recorded output figures'. This is, of course, particularly relevant to the building boom of the mid-thirties, and it is interesting to note that the Lomax index which *includes* building shows a 3·3 per cent per annum growth rate between 1924 and 1927, but if building is excluded the rate drops to 3 per cent per annum. This is a significant margin of difference even allowing for the undoubted impact of the building boom. Other industries in which sub-contracting was important were vehicles, certain branches of electrical goods, textiles, printing, clothing and leather. The overall consequence of this problem is, of course, twofold: it distorts fluctuations in the output of an industry over time, and it affects base-year weighting. In terms of the inter-war years it might be suggested that on balance it tends to inflate the importance of the so-called 'new' sectors.

There are, in addition, a number of other problems to which attention has been drawn: the improvement in the quality of information between 1900 and 1935, and particularly between 1924 and 1935, could well have the spurious effect of producing an acceleration in the rate of industrial production. Where it is necessary to rely on information supplied by a sample of firms, it is difficult to be certain of the representativeness of the sample: some estimates have been built up on assumptions concerning the relationship, in output terms, between large and small firms in an industry; the Lomax index is for the principal products, only, of individual industries. More generally, the Lomax index varies from other previous ones: the most striking difference is with the pre-war Board of Trade index which shows a growth rate of about half that of the Lomax index, and it differs to a lesser extent from the well-known Hoffmann index. This could well be the product of weighting and the choice of base years, but it seems to illustrate forcibly the problem of making precise calculations over short periods of time. And it emphasises the effects of an unavoidable margin of error on figures for growth rates which are absolutely of low orders of magnitude, but for which variations of $\frac{1}{2}$ per cent or 1 per cent are of very high cumulative significance.

The most difficult estimates of all are those for productivity. Consideration of this question brings one up against difficulties of changes in the quality of goods for which it is often virtually impossible to compensate, and changes in hours of work. Moreover, one needs to have a great deal of empirical information on individual industries before one can interpret productivity measures with any confidence. For example, the 'shake-out' effect of unemployment probably resulted in productivity gains quite independently of changes in techniques; and the good productivity record of agriculture during these years cannot be equated with growth and prosperity.

Finally, alternative methods of calculating gross domestic product figures illustrate the underlying weaknesses in the available data. Calculations based on expenditure data on the one hand and production data on the other give significantly different results. As an illustration of the effect which a small margin of error can have on the final growth rate, we have included the calculation shown in the bottom line of Table 1. This problem is reflected in national income series where the comparative rates of growth are as shown in Table 2. It seems likely that expenditure data are more reliable than income data, and this means that the probable growth rate for the economy during the inter-war period (by whichever yardstick it is measured) is nearer to the lower estimate than to the upper (Feinstein, 1964, xii).

Table 1

Rate of Growth of U.K. Gross Domestic Product, 1924–37

		Estimate based on output data	Estimate based on expenditure data
Index (1938 = 100)	1924	75·7	75·6
Index (1938 = 100)	1937	101·2	97·0
Rate of growth (per cent per annum)	1924–37	2·3	2·0
Rate of growth (per cent per annum) assuming 1937 is 5 per cent overestimated	1924–37	1·9	1·5

Source: Feinstein (1963, xii, Table I).

Table 2

Rate of Growth of U.K. Net National Income, 1924–37

		Estimate based on income data	Estimate based on expenditure data
Net national income at 1914 prices in £'000s	1924	2,147	2,284
Net national income at 1914 prices in £'000s	1937	2,986	3,019
Rate of growth (per cent per annum)	1924–37	2·6	2·2

Source: Feinstein (1964, ix, Table 1); Mitchell and Deane (1962, 478).

There remains one aspect of the statistical appraisal of the overall performance of the British economy between the wars to be considered, namely its comparative achievement within the longer-term growth pattern of the economy. On the basis of gross domestic product, the growth trend for the inter-war years is at least as good as that for 1870–1913. For industrial production alone, the record for the inter-war period is even better than that for the earlier period. And, taken together, these figures have led some commentators to argue that the years between 1918 and 1939 compare very favourably with those before 1914.

It may well be true that the late Victorian economy was not as buoyant as earlier writers have suggested, but the new orthodoxy

26

is probably wide of the mark in its evaluation of the longer-term performance of the British economy. There are a number of reasons why this is so. First, it has already been argued above that the accepted figures for growth in the inter-war years are probably overestimates. Secondly, Matthews (1964, Table I) and Dowie (1968, 97) have pointed out that there was a significant break in growth trends at around 1899–1900, which has the effect of pulling down the overall figures when the years 1870–1914 are considered as a piece. Thirdly, a somewhat similar

Table 3

Rate of Growth of U.K. Net National Income, Industrial Production and Gross Domestic Product, 1856–1913

(per cent per annum)

	Net national income at constant prices	*Industrial production index* (1913 = 100) (*excluding building*)	*Gross domestic product at constant prices*
1856–1899	2·9	2·2	2·0
1899–1913	0·8	1·9	1·1
1856–1913	2·3	2·1	n.a.

Source: C. H. Feinstein, 'Income and Investment in the United Kingdom, 1856–1914', *Economic Journal*, LXXI (1961), reprinted in Mitchell and Deane (1962, 367–8); Hoffman (1955, Table 54, part B); Matthews (1964, Table I).

downward bias in production series to that already commented on in respect of the inter-war years operates in the pre-1914 period, but with the opposite effect (Ashworth, 1966, 31); the net value weighting of the newer sectors of industry are underestimated because of rapidly falling unit costs (and thus final prices), mainly as the result of increasing economies of scale and the process of 'learning by doing'. Fourthly, and perhaps most importantly, interpretation of the pre-war years is clouded by the fact of an apparent marked difference between national income growth and production growth (see Table 3).

A large part of this difference is probably explained by a marked improvement in terms of trade over the late nineteenth

27

century, which helped to maintain real income growth even though the rate of growth of domestic production was falling off. Another factor was the rapid increase in net income from overseas investment, although in direct terms this should not be overemphasised; if overseas earnings are subtracted from national income figures, the overall growth rate of national income is reduced by 0·1 per cent per annum. Indirectly, however, the buoyancy of overseas earnings is indicative of the expansion of the service sector – both domestically and externally – during the quarter century or so before 1914.[5]

Ashworth (1966, 31) has pointed out that some discrepancy between income and gross production series arises because a rising proportion of the production figures represented 'value added in manufacture'; in other words, net output was rising faster than gross production and this 'real' gain is not reflected in the final production series. This can be put yet another way by saying that raw materials represented a declining proportion of the final value of goods produced. And in so far as the difference between income and production series for these years is the result of inadequate statistics, Feinstein has suggested that the major weakness in this respect is most likely to be an underestimate of the service sector in the production series.

In sum, therefore, it would seem that the purely statistical comparisons which have been drawn between the inter-war years and the period before 1914 should be modified in three ways: the rates of growth of production should be adjusted upwards for the pre-war years and downwards for the period 1918–39; the break in the growth trend at 1899–1900 should be clearly indicated; the overall performance of the economy in terms of national income, as distinct from the narrower measure of industrial production, is significantly higher over the period 1856–99 than over the inter-war years. But such comparisons can be made completely meaningful only if there exists some notion of the potential against which performance can be measured. And before this can be attempted, the nature of the inter-war economy needs to be considered in a little more detail. Yet one fact is immediately

[5] See, for example, Barry Supple, *The Royal Exchange Assurance* (Cambridge, 1970).

28

clear; however sophisticated and plausible are the arguments that seek to present the inter-war years as a period of economic progress, from 1923 to 1939 the official unemployment rate never fell below 10·0 per cent and at its highest, in 1932, it touched 22·5 per cent.

3 Monetary Policy and the Level of Investment

IT is appropriate to begin with some comments on monetary policy since, over the earlier part of the period, it was considered to be a major economic issue. Present discussion, however, will concentrate mainly on the period leading up to the return to gold in 1925, because it is this aspect of financial policy which is most commonly alleged to have affected the growth performance of the economy. It is attractive to depict this episode as one in which 'villainous' bankers, led by Montagu Norman, Governor of the Bank of England, dictated policy to successive governments regardless of its broader economic consequences, which they did not understand, and heedless of its social costs, which they considered to be unavoidable. And all the while they thwarted Keynes's efforts to persuade the Government to adopt an alternative course. And even when this charge is stripped of its polemics, there remains a substantial case against Norman and a small circle of Treasury officials and City bankers. Put simply, the argument is that restrictive monetary measures, which were aimed at restoring conditions suitable for the return of operation on the gold standard, created high unemployment and undermined the ability of the economy to adjust its industrial structure to the changed circumstances of the post-war years. This thesis has been recently supported by Pollard (1970) in a survey of financial policy between the wars.[6]

The broad lines of monetary policy are well covered in all the general books on the period and need not detain us here. The most detailed account of the events which led up to the return to gold has been given by Moggridge (1969), who has drawn on official papers which recently became available. Put briefly, how-

[6] Pollard's survey forms the introduction to a book which includes reprints of the articles by Sayers (1960) and Hume (1963).

ever, the facts are that the inflationary boom of the post-war years was getting out of hand by 1919 and the Government decided that it was necessary to apply the brakes. But what was a reasonable measure of good finance soon developed into a thoroughgoing deflationary policy. On the advice of the Cunliffe Committee the Government had in 1918 decided to return to gold and, in order to achieve this at the pre-war parity, this necessitated bringing British prices down into line with those of the United States, an operation which could only be achieved through severe credit restriction. This action was stepped up in 1921 when a Committee on National Expenditure (known as the Geddes Committee) was set up to recommend possible cuts in public expenditure; and soon the 'Geddes axe' was being wielded with ferocity. From 1922 onwards, however, deflationary pressure was very mild since the previous policy had proved to be a powerful depressant.

In the light of these facts, much of Pollard's argument seems incontrovertible. The rate at which Britain returned to gold in 1925 (at $4·86 to £1) was unreal in that it did not reflect the true situation in either domestic or international terms: it was purely artificial since it relied on the imposition of a number of restrictions on the free market situation. The Government, following its Treasury and City advisers, put the exchange before any consideration of its consequences for the domestic economy. Indeed, it is important, as Pollard says, to emphasise the extremely narrow representativeness of the bankers who were advising the Government through such bodies as the Cunliffe and Bradbury committees. Moreover, the Court of the Bank of England was itself made up almost entirely of men of the same ilk, and it was dominated by Norman who, on his own admission, allowed his actions to be guided by the 'feel' of the foreign exchange market. And it is abundantly clear from the cross-examination of Norman before the Macmillan Committee, a few years later, that he did not understand that the consequences of his own actions had a much broader effect on banking and finance than simply within the comparatively narrow foreign-exchange market. Norman's biographers paint a portrait of an autocratic, aloof man who, during the latter period of his office as Governor, suffered lapses

31

of mental stability; though it is remarkable that he remained as Governor long after his holy cow of the gold exchange rate had been sacrificed, and he did not resign his post until forced to do so in 1944, for reasons of health.

Naturally enough, critics have pointed to the apparent weakness of governments of differing labels in the face of the powerful interests of the Treasury and the City of London. As Pollard argues, however, this is not to represent financial policy as a 'bankers' ramp', but quite simply to argue that those in power believed, unreasonably so, in a capitalist system, that bankers acted in the public interest whilst the Government itself was incapable of producing any independent effective policy in so specialised a field. Moreover, Moggridge (1969) sees the return to pre-war parity as an act which had most serious repercussions on the viability of British industry in competition with foreign producers.

While accepting many of these strictures on financial policy up to 1931, other commentators, most notably Sayers (1960), Youngson (1967) and Clay (1957), have put forward some mitigating arguments from both an historical and an *ex-post* viewpoint. In particular, it has been observed that the return to gold at pre-war parity received general support and that Keynes was virtually alone in his condemnation of it.[7] Hume (1963) has shown, however, that there was a substantial body of 'respectable' opinion ranged against the line being followed over the early twenties. And although in the end it acquiesced in the return to gold, because it could see no workable alternative, it was consistently opposed to the degree of deflation operated in the economy over those years: common sense suggested that there was something inherently contradictory in measures which claimed to be restoring the health of the economy but which were patently damaging it at its most vulnerable point. Indeed Churchill, who as Chancellor of the Exchequer made the decision to return to gold, was impressed by Keynes's allusion to 'the paradox of unemployment in the midst of dearth', and in a memorandum to Sir Otto Niemeyer, his senior Treasury adviser who was utterly convinced on the need to return to gold

[7] Keynes's most effective attack was made in an essay *The Economic Consequences of Mr Churchill* (1925).

32

Churchill demanded whether there was not some alternative policy, observing: 'I would rather see Finance less proud and Industry more content.'[8]

While it is undoubtedly true that Keynes was not alone in criticising financial policy, he was, nevertheless, the leading advocate of alternative measures; but it is questionable whether he was an altogether effective advocate. For example, his earlier views on the reparations question, though brilliantly argued, had not commended themselves universally;[9] not least because of the sardonic and, not infrequently, contentious manner in which he approached public issues of this kind. Moreover, quite apart from the personality of Keynes, it would be wrong to assume that there was a clearly formulated alternative course of action being actively canvassed. It will be shown later how Keynes's views on this and other matters were still evolving, and his writings of the twenties and early thirties form, in many important respects, a lengthy prolegomena to his *General Theory* published in 1936. And Moggridge, somewhat contradictorily in view of his general argument in support of Keynes's consistency, shows how the arguments advanced by Keynes and McKenna before the Chamberlain–Bradbury Committee of 1924 contained significant ambiguities. For these reasons, therefore, it is necessary to modify Hume's conclusions.

Another plea in mitigation has been made along the lines that the Government was not clearly advised as to the extreme difficulty of making evaluations of relative international price levels, when determining the basis for the return. In such a very limited technical matter this could well have been the case; on the other hand the Government knew full well that it was endeavouring to create suitable conditions for the restoration of gold by means which were anything other than free market conditions of the kind that had operated before 1914. Nevertheless, it is quite clear that official thinking on the necessary price adjustments fluctuated with the floating exchange rate. Moreover, changes in the London bill market meant that the Bank operated under different

[8] Quoted by Moggridge (1969, 54).

[9] See John Maynard Keynes, *The Economic Consequences of the Peace* (1920).

conditions from those of 1914. The sterling bill, the credit instrument of international trade, had declined in relative importance, whereas short-term Treasury bills had flooded on to the market as a result of the needs of war finance.

More particularly in relation to the effect of the return to gold on the competitiveness of British industry, it has been suggested that the authorities' reasonable hopes and expectations were thwarted by extraneous factors, especially by the 'irresponsible' behaviour of other countries – most notably France and Belgium – that followed a policy of competitive devaluation. If so, then at best the British were ingenuous, at worst they still believed that the City of London was the all-powerful centre of the financial world. Certainly, there is ample evidence that the British authorities were living in a make-believe pre-1914 world. They did not understand how the emergence of New York as a major financial centre necessitated changes in banking policy which were not called for by the strict balance of payments position. In particular, this aspect of Norman's failings has been explored by Williams (1959).

Having considered the manner of the return to gold, it is now possible to question whether monetary policy in support of that act was a major factor in the performance of the British economy during the 1920s. Obviously, any analysis of this issue involves *ex-post* reasoning. Pollard argues that the deflation had enormously damaging effects on those sectors of the economy experiencing the worst conditions of depression. Moggridge lays particular emphasis on the competitive disadvantage suffered by British industry through the overvaluation of the pound, by about 10·0 per cent. Sayers, who first raised the question, takes a somewhat different view by arguing that a 10·0 per cent reduction in the gold/dollar parity would have had little effect on the depressed staple sectors which had suffered a decline in exports, since the plain truth was that the French were determined to maintain their exchange-rate advantage and that British industry was suffering directly from a resurgence of German competition. The balance of evidence seems to be firmly on Sayers's side, though it is necessary to distinguish the effects of the exchange rate from the effects of the period of deflation which preceded it; for it could be argued that this latter was the really damaging part of the whole operation.

In support of his thesis Moggridge shows that although German unit wage costs in manufacturing industry were rising quite rapidly from 1925 onwards, the Germans still retained a competitive advantage over this country until 1929, because of the favourable rate at which the mark had been set against the pound in 1925. However, Kindleberger in 1956 calculated that a 10·0 per cent devaluation of sterling would have lowered export prices by only 5·8 per cent.[10] Moreover, Moggridge draws his wage data from Phelps Brown and Browne, and these show that on the eve of the return to gold German unit wage costs in manufacturing industry were very substantially below those ruling in Britain, because of the major restructuring of German prices after the hyper-inflation of the early twenties. In other words, it would appear that the gap that Britain had to close was significantly wider than anything which could be achieved by a 10·0 per cent devaluation. Furthermore, from the evidence cited by Phelps Brown and Browne and Moggridge, Britain's competitive position vis-à-vis other major economies in general would seem to have been even weaker than it was against Germany.[11]

More fundamentally, however, there are big questions hanging over the assumptions that Moggridge makes about the price elasticity of demand for British exports in the 1920s. It is quite

[10] See C. P. Kindleberger, *The Terms of Trade* (Cambridge, Mass., 1956) pp. 97–8.

[11] See Phelps Brown and Browne (1968, 221–34 and Appendix 3). Unit wage cost is a measure for relating wages and productivity. The figures show that in 1924–5 the gap between Britain and Germany in terms of unit wage costs was of the order of 15·0 per cent on the basis of the comparative unit wage costs position of the two countries in 1913. While comparative calculations of this kind are open to criticism – particularly in relation to possible differences in costs other than wage costs between the countries concerned – they are accurate enough for the purpose in question. In short, if the 15·0 per cent difference in unit wage costs gave the Germans, in effect, only a 10·0 per cent export price advantage, it would have required approximately a 17·0 per cent devaluation by Britain to remove that advantage.

unsatisfactory to move from average calculations of the kind just considered, and from similar general data and statistical analyses relating to international trade over very long periods, to assumptions about the competitiveness of, and relative price elasticities of demand for, the types of goods which Britain was attempting to trade internationally in the 1920s.[12] Discussion on the subject of British industry and the performance of these exports, in the following sections, suggests that this price elasticity was very low. Correspondingly, it will be argued that a falling off in British invisible earnings was not mainly determined by the factors of price elasticity.

The argument for freer credit in the early twenties rests on the *a priori* assumption that short-term monetary policies provide the key to long-term economic growth. Certainly, modern economic theory and economic experience since the Second World War indicate that the relationship between the money supply and the level of economic activity, and between the rate of interest and the level of investment, is both disputed and by no means self-evident.[13] There are those who argue that the money stock has a direct and powerful influence on the level of growth and others who lay stress on the composition and availability of the money supply. Nevertheless, there is a fair level of agreement that monetary policy is more effective in controlling booms than in stimulating recovery from depression, and this principle would tend to tell against its potential effectiveness in the early 1920s. Moreover, recent European experience does not support the view that high interest rates are necessarily a drag on investment, and anyway, after 1921 interest rates were quite low and the evidence

[12] A study of the evidence cited by Moggridge (1969, 115 n. 26, 118 n. 1) in support of his assumptions, fully illustrates the criticism made above. And his assumption (p. 91) that 'all other things remain equal' seems most unrealistic.

[13] In these connections see Robert W. Clower, *Monetary Theory: Selected Readings* (1969); David R. Croome and H. G. Johnson, *Money in Britain, 1959–1969* (1969); B. R. Williams, *International Report on Investment Behaviour* (O.E.C.D., Paris, 1962); M. M. Postan, *An Economic History of Western Europe, 1945–1964* (1967) chap. 5.

36

suggests that monetary policy did not act as a hindrance to the supply of finance through the stock market or the commercial banks.[14]

More generally, it is open to serious question whether much freer monetary conditions, or even a more thoroughgoing kind of Keynesian policy, would have achieved success during the twenties. Even today economists disagree among themselves as to whether short-term equilibrium policies of this nature provide the fundamental means of creating an economic climate in which long-term growth can occur smoothly and satisfactorily; and this is in the context of a general acceptance of the aim of full, or near-full, employment and of a much greater all-round understanding of the necessary conditions for economic growth than existed in the 1920s. Against this there is convincing evidence – which is considered in the next section – that the fundamental growth problem of the economy in the inter-war years was a structural one, and that under those conditions the alternative policy outlined by Pollard and Moggridge would at best have been a palliative, at worst an irritant. It must be emphasised, however, that these observations relate solely to monetary policy and do not imply any assumption by the Government of a much more direct intervention in economic affairs. This is important because there is a tendency on the part of those who lay stress on monetary policy to support their arguments, unconsciously no doubt, by assumptions of a more positive government role which is not at all a necessary condition of such a policy and is, indeed, part of a quite different question.

Without in any way seeking to minimise the failure of financial policy in the twenties, the foregoing review suggests that when judged in historical terms there does not appear to have been any clearly expressed alternative. And this fact might give a little credence to those who support the view that the return did, at least, bring certain positive advantages : it helped to keep down import prices; it gave exchange stability which did something to help business confidence; and it made some contribution to international stability for five years or so. But more importantly, it

[14] See T. Balogh, *Studies in Financial Organisation* (1947) p. 75.

seems doubtful whether it was of more than marginal significance in Britain's economic difficulties.

The denouement came in 1931 when Britain abandoned the gold standard. It is both ironic and revealing that the May Report of July 1931 should have contributed to a 'flight from the pound'. Ironic, because the May Committee, which had been charged to recommend 'all possible reductions in the National Expenditure on supply services', lived up to the tradition of Cunliffe and Geddes by condemning public extravagance and preaching economy and retrenchment; and this, combined with its gloomy budget forecast, helped to cause a failure of confidence in the pound. Orthodoxy thus contained the seeds of its own destruction. Revealing, because although the May Report was intellectually bankrupt as an analysis of the country's economic ills, it carried a much clearer message and a more easily assimilated programme for action than the Macmillan Report which appeared in the following month.[15] This is not to excuse the authorities for acting on the May Committee's proposals for swingeing cuts in public expenditure, particularly in the social services, but it does reveal something of the relationship between economic analysis, practical politics and economic policy.

After a short period of tight money the Government introduced a 'cheap money' policy primarily for reasons of reducing debt charges and deterring speculative investment from London. The external exchange now found its equilibrum against gold-bloc countries; and having established the Exchange Equalisation Account in 1932 – which, by means of a fund of Treasury bills, foreign currency and gold, was operating successfully to protect the pound – the Government adopted 'cheap money' as a new orthodoxy. Most commentators agree that this was a permissive rather than an active factor in the improvement of the economy from 1933 onwards – a fact which leads one to question, yet again, how effective easier money would have been in solving the economic problems of the 1920s. Its most positive effect was most probably in encouraging the flow of investment into residential construction in the mid-thirties and, as will be suggested, the

[15] The 'star performers' on the Macmillan Committee were, of course, Keynes and Bevin.

overall effects of this on economic growth might not have been altogether salutary (see below, p. 49).

Because of the passions which the financial issues of this period have aroused in the past, it is perhaps easy to overlook their wider implications. Many writers have pointed out that it would be more accurate to describe the pre-1914 exchange system as a sterling standard rather than a gold standard; and it was not until the inter-war years that the gold standard was put to the full test – and found wanting. But the erection of something to take its place was not something that Britain could accomplish on its own; although Norman and his associates undoubtedly believed this to be possible – at least until 1931. Thus there were limits to which Britain could go in putting its own financial system in order so long as international financial co-operation remained unattainable. The tragedy was that autarky, which infected the international economy in the 1930s, provided an insulation to the British economy and thus, in effect, reduced the pressure on the authorities to search for some new alternative. It is possible that this helped to preserve many cherished attitudes towards sterling and its role in the world financial system which found expression again after the Second World War and which produced conditions that have acted as a drag on Britain's growth performance ever since.

Discussion of monetary policy leads on to consideration of the behaviour of longer-term capital investment. Indeed, one of the most interesting links between the financial system and capital investment was made by the Macmillan Committee (1931, 161–74) when it drew unfavourable comparisons between Britain on the one hand and Germany, the United States and France on the other, on the relationship between banks and industry. And the lack of such a positive relationship in Britain for the provision of capital for small and medium-sized firms became known as the 'Macmillan Gap'. The real extent of this gap – if indeed there was one – has never been investigated in any detail, though it is fairly clear that the commercial banks needed to improve their expertise in this field considerably if they were to play the role recommended for them by the Macmillan Committee.

It is impossible to say whether this factor caused a shortage of available capital in the 1930s. It has been shown, for example, that the banks indirectly provided certain industries with liquid funds for new investment by purchasing fixed-interest securities which many large firms had held in their reserve portfolios. But to what extent demands for loans were not met, or to what extent businessmen (particularly smaller ones) were unwilling to seek loans because of the banks' traditional attitude to long-term investment, is not known. Moreover, the picture is complicated by the growth of intermediate agencies in the 1920s and 1930s – particularly in the realm of investment trusts and credit finance – which were often very dependent on banks for their resources. At the same time there was rapid growth in insurance companies that had very large funds to invest on the open market, especially in the 1930s. In addition, the lack of business in foreign trade caused the acceptance houses to turn their attention to providing services for domestic industry. In short, Grant's description (1937) of the capital market in the 1930s suggests that the system itself was not inefficient. On the other side, the success of new issues on the market suggests that capital was forthcoming for operations of this kind.

The pattern of total investment, however, is fairly clear and far less impressive. Feinstein's estimates (see source to Table 4 below) show that gross capital formation as a percentage of national income fell off in the inter-war years compared with the pre-war period, and this can be broken down into constituent elements: domestic investment, excluding dwellings, remained fairly constant; foreign investment fell away sharply; and this fall was not made up by the sharp rise in investment in dwellings.

Net investment figures are far less reliable because of problems of estimating depreciation, but for what they are worth, the picture they give is fairly dismal for the inter-war years: between 1922 and 1924 and between 1931 and 1933, for example, there was actually disinvestment in manufacturing. In terms of innovation, however, gross investment is more appropriate because since the First World War it is probably true to say that a great deal of innovation has been embodied in replacement of existing plant and machinery. Moreover, in so far as this was the case, it

40

implies that the 'age' of capital equipment was becoming less of a burden for an older industrial country, such as Great Britain, in comparison with its 'newer' competitors. In other words, as obsolescence became the dominant reason for investment, a declining proportion of Britain's gross domestic investment was being committed to the maintenance of existing capital; and to this extent the competitive disadvantage which Britain suffered from having an old industrial structure was lessened.

Table 4

U.K. Investment as a Percentage of Gross National Product, Selected Decades, 1900–59

(annual rates at current prices)

	1900–9	1920–9	1930–8	1950–9
A. £m. at current prices				
1. G.N.P. at factor cost	2,000	4,620	4,440	16,540
B. Percentage of G.N.P. at factor cost				
2. Total investment	13·3	12·0	10·5	18·0
3. Gross domestic fixed capital formation				
(a) Dwellings	1·5	2·3	3·4	3·4
(b) Other	6.9	6·7	6·9	13·0
4. Net investment abroad	4·4	2·1	−0·6	0·6
5. Stockbuilding	0·5	0·9	0·8	1·0
6. Net domestic fixed capital formation	n.a.	2·2	3·2	n.a.

Source: C. H. Feinstein, *Domestic Capital Formation in the United Kingdom, 1920–1938* (Cambridge, 1965) pp. 36, 49.

In view of the overall figures it is difficult to accept that difficulties in the staple industries resulted in very marked transfer of resources to new growth sectors. The new sectors of industry were, as is so frequently pointed out, relatively capital-intensive when compared with the old staple industries. Therefore, if these sectors had been making a major contribution to overall industrial growth, in either the twenties or the thirties, it would be reasonable to expect a disproportionate rise in aggregate capital investment. Clearly, this did not occur. It is possible, of course, that despite an overall negative net investment in manufacturing

41

in the early thirties there were significant sectoral shifts within the total investment pattern in those directions, and this might well have acted as a stabilising factor; but in aggregate it still does not appear to have been enough to promote more rapid growth. More generally, Feinstein (op. cit., 40–8) shows that there is no significant correlation between investment cycles and general cycles in the economy.

These features of capital investment are particularly related to what was happening in the foreign sector. It is important to realise that a proportion of overseas investment before 1914 indirectly formed part of the capital–output ratio for the whole economy : the level of output of many domestic industries depended on foreign demand stimulated by British overseas investment. If, therefore, the shape of the British economy had to change in the direction of a larger proportionate concentration on the domestic market – a point which will be elaborated in the next section – then it was all the more necessary that funds which would previously have gone abroad should have found their way into domestic channels. That they did not do so is a clear indication of an inherent weakness in the inter-war economy.

Why did they not do so? This is a major question to which, as yet, no one has produced a satisfactory answer. So far as the pre-war economy is concerned, doubts have been raised as to the efficiency of the capital market for directing capital into domestic industry; whereas the opposite is alleged to have been true of the foreign securities market. This weakness could have continued into the inter-war years, but from what has been said it is difficult to maintain that this was true in the 1930s. And even if this is assumed to have been the case, two further questions are raised. How important should one rate the new issue market as a source of new domestic investment? If it did suffer from the shortcomings which have been mentioned, to what extent was this a failure in its own organisation as against a lack of demand from domestic industry for a more efficient market? As to the first question, the obvious point to make is that ploughed-back profits have always been the major source of industrial investment. And, to repeat an earlier observation, the new issue market seems to have been reasonably efficient in the 1930s. The second question is, by implication, considered more fully in the next section. But it has to be said at once that it cannot be fully resolved until a great deal more information is available on the history of individual business enterprises. On the basis of such studies as have been produced, a guess might be hazarded : firms which were turning to the production of 'newer' goods probably enjoyed high enough profit returns to finance their desired level of investment; for firms facing major problems of contraction and reorganisation, shortage of capital was probably a secondary consequence and/or of secondary importance to management efficiency, company structure and government policy.

It is possible to make rough estimates of the contributions of capital and labour to economic growth; and the amount of growth which cannot be linked directly to capital and labour inputs is known as the 'residual' : the residual is, in short, the measure of unknown sources of growth, among which 'technical progress' is likely to be the most important. Now there are many limitations to this kind of analysis, and it is immediately obvious that one of them is the embodied relationship between capital inputs and associated technical progress. Nevertheless, despite such weaknesses, it does give us some insight into the growth process. Matthews (1964) has made calculations of this kind for the periods 1924–37 and 1948–62, and these suggest that if the rate of capital accumulation in the former period had matched the higher rate which was achieved between 1948 and 1962, then the rate of growth of gross domestic product between the wars would have been significantly higher than the recorded 2·3 per cent.

It is necessary to note, however, that the relationship between capital investment and growth is very far from clear. At the theoretical level and the empirical level there is marked disagreement among economists.[16] And although nearly all this contro-

[16] See Postan, *Economic History of Western Europe*. For the 'pro' and 'con' views on the importance of investment, see A. Maddison, *Economic Growth in the West* (1964) esp. chap. iii, and N. Kaldor, 'Capital Accumulation and Economic Growth', in *The Theory of Capital*, International Economic Association Conference (1961) pp. 177–222.

versy relates to the post-Second World War period, it emphasises the extreme difficulty in drawing any firm conclusions for the inter-war years. Therefore, we cannot answer which had to come first, but it is possible to throw some light on why neither was achieved; and at least, high investment is a necessary symptom of rapid growth. Thus, all one can say at the moment is that significantly higher growth in the inter-war period could not have occurred independently of a higher level of investment.

4 Factors in Business Enterprise and Efficiency

COMMENTATORS, from the Balfour Committee of the late twenties onwards, have pointed to the growth of major new sectors in industry during the inter-war years. Motor-vehicle production increased rapidly, though not evenly, from 1922 onwards; and in 1930 Britain became the largest producer of passenger and motor vehicles in Europe, by overtaking France which until then had led the field. This growth was associated with a marked fall in prices – by nearly 50 per cent between 1924 and 1937 – while the average factory price of all cars produced fell from £259 in 1924 to £130 in 1935. Rayon production shot up during the 1920s and the total continued to grow, though less rapidly, during the 1930s. The electrical industry contains a number of branches and there is therefore no really satisfactory over-all measure of its performance. Nevertheless, there are ample data available to illustrate the various aspects of the industry's expansion. For example, the number of cookers sold rose from 75,000 in 1930 to 250,000 by 1935, while the number of radio receivers increased from around half a million in 1930 to nearly two million by 1937. And, as with cars, production of these consumer goods was accompanied by a marked fall in prices. Moreover, an important factor in this growth was the enormous improvement in the efficiency of electricity generation, which had been achieved largely as a result of the establishment of the National Grid in 1926. And in addition to the foregoing industries, we might add the advances which were made in the fields of chemicals, aluminium, rubber, films, aircraft and food processing.

The broad features of these developments are, therefore, clear enough, but so often this evidence of growth of 'new' industries is presented in an uncritical fashion with little attempt being made to place it in perspective. For one thing, it should not be forgotten that we are dealing with a period of over twenty years, and it would be somewhat remarkable if there had not been some

45

noticeable technical advances over that time. But before we look at these developments in a little more detail, it will clarify the picture somewhat if we look generally at industrial structure between the wars.

The major staple industries of coal, textiles, iron and steel, and shipbuilding were massively depressed during these years, and one obvious major reason for this was the loss of overseas markets. More detailed observations on external trade will be made shortly, but for the moment it is important to note just how dependent on foreign markets the staple industries were. For example, just before the war the cotton textile industry exported 80 per cent, by value, of its total production of yarn and cotton piece goods; the figures for coal and iron and steel were one-third and 50·0 per cent respectively. Coal was probably worst affected since it experienced the stimulus of a sharp rise in European demand in 1923, because of the occupation of the Ruhr; but once the Ruhr coalfield began working normally, the British coal industry suffered a very sharp set-back and its exports dropped away to a low, stagnant level. Coal was also affected by the longer-term shift in demand to other fuels, the most important of which was oil, and this alone forced on the industry a major problem of structural adjustment.

Another obvious feature was the localised nature of the depression in the staple industries, which is most strikingly illustrated by the heavy unemployment associated with it. Yet the contrast between the depressed areas and other parts of the country can be painted a little too vividly. The southern counties, for instance, contained pockets of depression, most particularly in the agricultural industry; and even in the worst depressed areas there were bright patches. For example, because of differences in demand for different types of coal, the Scottish, Northumberland, Durham and Welsh coalfields were more depressed than those of Yorkshire and the Midlands. In textiles, the woollen industry managed some recovery in the 1930s. And both the cotton and shipbuilding industries experienced booms in certain sections under the fillip of the rearmament programme of the late 1930's. However, as a contemporary report pointed out in regard to the last factor : 'Indeed the position has been made worse in that re-adjustment towards changed conditions will have to start again from a higher level once the abnormal increase in demand for the products of certain industries has passed. The heavy industries of the depressed areas have been stimulated beyond their normal post-war level of activity ` . . .' (British Association, 1938, 111).

Another way of looking at the structure of industry is to look at the distribution of the labour force. According to recent calculations made by W. A. Cole there was no significant alteration in the rate of structural change – measured in terms of employment and net output per head – in the inter-war years.[17] In other words the so-called 'older' industries still bulked large in the economy or, alternatively, the so-called 'new' industries did not constitute such a large sector of industry as to be a powerful driving force of expansion. Indeed, the constant and relatively low rate of labour mobility into the higher-productivity sectors of industry operated as a drag on the economy. And the building industry, which experienced among the highest gains in employment between 1924 and 1937, was characterised by low levels of output per man. Moreover, Dowie's calculations (1968, 109, 111) show that this relative position as between industries is similarly reflected in terms of capital stock. For example, in 1937 electrical engineering, motor vehicles, and rayon and silk accounted for 1·5 per cent of the total capital stock or 9·7 per cent of the capital stock of manufacturing industry. The corresponding figures for cotton textiles alone were 1·3 per cent and 8·4 per cent and, moving outside manufacturing industry, mining and quarrying accounted for 2·7 per cent of total capital stock.

There is enough evidence to indicate that to some extent, at least, the problems facing the basic industries were beyond the powers of individual entrepreneurs to solve. In a spirited defence of the coal-owners, Buxton (1970) has argued that factors of

[17] These observations are derived from the paper which W. A. Cole gave at the International Conference of Economic History at Leningrad in 1970, 'Changes in British Industrial Structure, 1850–1960'; the method used by Cole is a development of that employed by W. Ashworth in 'Changes in Industrial Structure, 1870–1914', *Yorkshire Bulletin of Economic and Social Research,* xvii (1965).

demand, operating costs and capital structure severely limited the mine-owners' freedom of manœuvre in response to depressed markets. This probably goes too far in exonerating the owners when one bears in mind their attitudes and views expressed before successive investigations into the industry and during the General Strike. Nevertheless, the general point of the inability of a private industry to achieve major changes in its structural organisation which would have contributed to its own and the economy's longer-term growth, however high the calibre of its entrepreneurs, is one worthy of further investigation in relation to other depressed sectors. In short, in so far as British industry exhibited a degree of 'over-commitment' of resources to its less productive sectors, in certain respects it was probably a matter for central action rather than something to be left to the 'forces of the market'.

Closely allied to the foregoing discussion is the question of industrial location. Apart from general analysis of the distribution of industry during the inter-war years, this is a sadly neglected subject. In part, at least, this is probably because the problem has been seen more in terms of unemployment and its relief, rather than in relation to the longer-term growth of the economy. The contrast between the depressed regions and the more prosperous ones has already been drawn, but it would be wrong to assume from this that there was a simple and basically rational relocation of industry occurring in the inter-war years. Sometimes newer branches of industry were developed in certain areas for no apparent reason – as, for example, the establishment of the major part of rayon manufacture at Coventry. More often, developments occurred in certain places because they grew out of old-established craft trades. This is illustrated by the association between the new motor-vehicle industry and the older coach-building industry, in London and the South-east; Saul (1962) has shown how the original location of the motor-vehicle industry in the Midlands area was similarly conditioned by a number of accidental factors. Dennison (1939), in his pioneering study of location, laid considerable emphasis on the close availability of a large market, and this factor was also stressed by the Barlow Commission (1940); nevertheless, accruing evidence would suggest that in strict economic terms proximity to markets was not a prime necessity, and it is very questionable whether it was a major influence in originally determining the location of new branches of manufacturing industry. There were, moreover, less obvious factors : among the reasons for the heavy concentration of various branches of the electrical industry in London were the early establishment there (in the 1830s) of cable manufacture for the electric telegraph and the availability of skilled men from the declining Clerkenwell watch and clock industry who were ideally trained for the manufacture of electric meters and similar equipment.

Undoubtedly, growth in these areas reached a point where it usually produced external economies to the individual firm and therefore represented a rational choice by the individual entrepreneur. But when this is considered in relation to the new infrastructure which developed in association with it, one may question whether this growth was producing external economies to the economy as a whole. Many have argued, with reason, that the building boom of the mid-thirties was, if not the major factor, then a powerful one in encouraging an upswing in the economy; but should one not question whether it imposed longer-term diseconomies on the economy as a whole? It is only necessary to reflect upon the enormous costs of congestion generated in certain major areas of the country since the Second World War to draw attention to the soundness, or otherwise, of developments which occurred in the inter-war years. The net result of this might be to suggest that, for longer-term economic benefit, growth points of industry should have been located in other areas; or, at least, it suggests that the developments they gave rise to should have been more directly controlled.

More than one economic historian has illustrated the paradox, in the 1930s, of labour shortage in relatively booming areas of the country combined with heavy unemployment in the depressed regions. In part, this reflects differences in age structure and employment opportunities. In part also, it reflects the problem of the distribution of stock of social overhead capital, particularly as represented by working-class housing, and its redistribution in relation to changes in industrial location. At the same time, however, the relocation of industry during this period amounted to a shift in balance and not a complete change from one pattern to another. In other words, recovery could never be complete, in the sense of establishing the basis for rapid long-term growth, until the major staple industries had achieved thorough-going innovation of their operations. These industries, in particular iron and steel, would necessarily continue to account for a large proportion of economic resources. But in attempting to make such adjustments these industries were to some extent prisoners of a pattern of infrastructure which had been developed to match their pre-war roles. Perhaps of most importance in this respect was the pattern of transport services (this is discussed at pp. 70–1 below).

Finally, in this respect, the ability of any one industry to overcome its difficulties was weakened by the widespread nature of depression in industry and the more general forces of economic depression. At the general level this was a complex mixture of cause and effect; but at the level of the industry or the firm widespread economic depression sapped confidence and led to an easy preference for excuses over action. Thus the evidence suggests that the process of structural change in British industry operated within a framework which in many important respects was either too restrictive or too permissive to permit satisfactory development. In Section 6 it is suggested that the only satisfactory solution to this problem lay with the Government adopting a more positive economic policy (see pp. 65–72). At the same time, however, this does not preclude a large measure of individual responsibility for the efficiency, or otherwise, with which business enterprises in all sections of the economy responded to the problems and opportunities of the inter-war period. Moreover, the total effect of greater success in this direction than was in fact achieved might well have removed, or eased, some of the general constraints which have been alluded to. And, it might be speculated, if the business community had shown more vigour on its own behalf, the Government in its turn might have been led to more appropriate action in economic affairs than it actually adopted.

The record of technical advance in the 1920s and 1930s has

been described by Sayers (1950), and the achievements of enterprise and innovation based on those advances have been extolled by Aldcroft (1966) and Richardson (1961). But one of the dangers implicit in the latter approach is that of defining business enterprise solely in terms of technical innovation while forgetting that it involves a number of other, equally important, elements. One factor which immediately springs to mind is that of British industry's efficiency in the field of marketing. It has been suggested that there were weaknesses here that stemmed from the pre-war period when the major British industries enjoyed a quasi-monopolistic position in international markets. Accruing evidence does not altogether support this view, however, since it provides examples of the flexibility and ingenuity of British manufacturers in tapping new sources of overseas demand before the First World War. Moreover, although in some markets, mainly in Asia, Britain had retained an enormous proportion of the trade, there were few in which Britain faced no threat of competition. Rather, it may well be the case that the marketing expertise developed in relation to the needs of a far from homogeneous international market was not suited, nor indeed adapted, to the exploitation of a large domestic market.

What is particularly interesting is the manner in which, in the most advanced sectors of British industry, developments in marketing techniques had not matched technical innovation. For example, in motor-car production, 'in 1937 the six leading British producers, making roughly 350,000 private cars, turned out more than forty different engine types and an even greater number of chassis and body models, which was considerably more than the number offered by the three leading producers in the United States, making perhaps 3,500,000 cars' (Kahn, 1946, 112–13). Other examples can be cited. Coleman (1969, chaps ix and xiii) has shown how Courtaulds, the leading British producer of rayon, was noticeably deficient in its marketing policy in the 1930s. In the electricity industry, although the generation of power had become highly efficient in organisation, the distribution and marketing of power was near-chaotic. In the tobacco industry, the gap between technical achievement and marketing proficiency widened noticeably in the 1930s. Quite

51

how far this kind of weakness was a feature of other industries cannot be judged through want of evidence; and the question is further complicated by the problem of the relationship between the distribution of income and the extent of a mass consumer market. It is significant, however, that as early as 1927 the Balfour Committee (chaps iii and v) drew attention, in general terms, to the need for closer regard to marketing and to the possibility of introducing greater standardisation in sizes and measurements of goods.

The nature of company organisation was another source of weakness in industry. One of the most comprehensive analyses of this problem has been provided by Sturmey (1962) in his study of shipping. But it is amply corroborated by evidence from other quarters: it was true of cotton, rayon, motor vehicles, electrical goods, chemicals, tobacco, coal, iron and steel, and shipbuilding. Moreover, it involved a number of interrelated problems. First there were those industries – such as cotton and iron and steel – that contained too many individual units for overall efficient organisation. This was not infrequently the product of firms having adopted limited liability – particularly in the late nineteenth century – for the benefits of greater security and greater supplies of capital, but at the same time having retained family control. Leek and Maizels (1945) have shown how the degree of concentration in a number of the staple industries was low. For example, in 1935 in cotton spinning the three largest units accounted for only 26 per cent of output; whereas, by contrast, at the other end of the scale the figure was 73 per cent in rubber tyres and tubes. One consequence of this was the growth of market-sharing and price-fixing arrangements, especially in the 1930s, which probably did not contribute a great deal to more efficient rationalisation of production. Too often these arrangements were merely defensive moves, as when shipping companies ran for cover in the conference system. Moreover, closely linked to the size of companies was the problem of over-capitalisation in the form of a heavy weight of fixed-interest liabilities, which frequently obscured the true financial position of an enterprise. Iron and steel provides the classic example of this: fixed-interest capital was used to purchase a large amount of obsolescent plant during the post-war boom, and when the boom collapsed the industry found itself being dragged under by this financial dead-weight. Or again, Wilson's study of Unilever (1954, 1 243–312) shows how serious a matter this became in the company in the 1920s – a company, moreover, which in many respects was in the 'new' category. More broadly, the Balfour Committee (1928, 20–3, 169–94) devoted detailed attention to the whole problem of over-capitalisation.

Industrial structure and business organisation were related in a cause-and-effect manner to the quality of management. This is an extremely complex issue in which, to varying degrees in different cases, a number of factors played a part : the degree of family control; the individual ability of entrepreneurs to formulate clear and accurate assessments of their enterprises; the restrictions on their ability to do so within the confines of an uneconomic organisation; the general fortunes of the industry; and the shortage of trained personnel at all levels. Industrial combination, or amalgamation, might well have done something to rationalise organisation and management, but until a great deal more research is done in this field it is impossible to draw any clear conclusions. At the moment, however, the available evidence does not present a very optimistic picture. In shipping, amalgamations often proved to be acts of desperation which had no basic economic rationale. In tobacco, it occurred as a purely defensive move – probably unnecessary – against international competition. But in both cases it took a long time to evolve efficient management structures within the large companies which had been created; though the consequences of this were considerably less in the tobacco industry than in shipping. It would be interesting to know what were the corresponding effects in other large companies formed in this way.

At another level, consideration of company organisation and management illustrates how meaningless it is to define 'new' industries simply in terms of technical innovation. To some degree it is probably true that concentration of business was the product of technical economies of scale, but the nature of the organisation associated with this was by no means necessarily 'new'. In the case of Courtaulds, for example, it has been shown how weaknesses

53

in this field, which sprang from personal foibles and traditional methods, had an increasingly deleterious effect on the company's progress over the 1930s. Moreover, the pioneering manner in which the motor industry evolved led to over-importance being given to the role of engineer at the expense of good management. It would be incorrect to argue that, in this latter case, the consequences were serious in the 1930s; but in so far as the industry's development at that time helped to determine its long-term growth, it is a factor of weight.

The lack of enthusiasm for management training on the part of British industry was commented on by the Balfour Committee (1927, 27): 'The fact, however, that the demand for higher commercial teaching of university rank has emanated rather from economists and educational observers than from the representatives of commerce does not substantially weaken the case for such education, for almost exactly the same observation could have been made a generation ago with regard to forms of technical and scientific education which have now become firmly established.' There is no evidence, however, of a thoroughgoing change in this attitude before 1939; and there was little attempt on the part of government to do anything to encourage such a change. Moreover, though the Balfour Report records some progress in technical education, it showed concern over the supply of individuals with the highest technical training: for example, while there was no shortage of engineers in the iron and steel industry, there was a shortage of metallurgists. To the extent that this was a general feature of industry it had significant repercussions. The latest methods of organisation and management tended to be associated with the most up-to-date technical processes. At one level such innovation produced simplification of problems since it replaced trained operatives and managers of long practical experience, with semi-skilled and unskilled operatives and workshop supervisors; but at the upper level it required highly trained technologists to control and direct total operations. In so far as the supply of such men was limited, fundamental innovation was restricted.

Allied to the shortage of highly trained scientific personnel in industry was the whole matter of industrial research. Again, there

54

is much contemporary criticism in this respect. Although a number of scientific research organisations were set up after the war by both government and industry, the indications are that, even by the end of the period, the amount of money spent in this field was still quite inadequate to the needs of industry.[18] Nevertheless, it is perhaps easy to overestimate the effect of this, since the problem in British industry in the inter-war years was not so much the discovery of new techniques – for even if they were made abroad they were usually universally available under licence – as in the willingness to innovate on the basis of them. Accordingly, the more immediate shortcoming than lack of research was, once again, the lack of personnel who were adequately trained to appraise the commercial value of technical advances, whatever their country of origin.

This latter fact partly explains the slow growth in output of certain new goods. Despite the rapid expansion of the motor industry, for example, the machine-tools it required were imported from abroad, and it was only under the stimulus of the re-armament programme of the late thirties that this deficiency was beginning to be made up. Other examples, in the field of household goods, are given by the more sophisticated electrical equipment such as electric cookers and electric water heaters; at best, production of these goods has been described as only 'promising' at the end of the period. However, as will be seen, the size of output of consumer durables was not simply determined by supply factors.

In the most general terms, the task facing the British economy in the inter-war period has been most clearly expressed by Ashworth: in the face of the inevitably changing distribution of economic power in the international economy and the increasing complexity of technological development, it was necessary to achieve a new structure of international specialisation in which 'countries of moderate size, like Britain and Germany, would concentrate particularly on the manufacture of high-quality goods, including most that require very advanced technique and equipment' (Ashworth, 1960, 315). A corollary of this was that,

[18] See Sir H. Frank Heath and A. L. Heatherington, *Industrial Research and Development in the United Kingdom: A Survey* (1945).

55

given the international distribution of income, a proportionately larger amount of resources would have to be devoted to production for the domestic market, while external trade would continue to grow absolutely even though its proportionate role would probably fall. Evidence of Britain's real achievements in this direction is clear enough in terms of shifts in employment and capital stocks; but it is equally obvious that in aggregate terms the achievement was far from optimum. The growth rate of industrial production was not high and the staple industries, which left a lot to be desired in terms of optimum efficiency, still bulked large in the economy.

The above survey has suggested that, so far as business organisation in a very wide sense was concerned, the explanation of the level of performance which was achieved is to be found in a combination of factors which in part were beyond the individual control of entrepreneurs and in part were the results of shortcomings for which they were in the main, though not entirely, responsible. But in the existing state of knowledge it would be extreme folly to assume that the reasons for this performance are clearly understood. Perhaps the largest unknown is formed by that group of industries broadly defined as the service and distribution sector; yet together they accounted for 46 per cent of total employment in 1937. Indeed, Matthews (1964, 17–18) has advanced the hypothesis that under the pressure of unemployment there was a concentration of underemployed labour in services and distribution. The implications of this hypothesis, if it is valid, are considerable. And, moreover, this sector witnessed considerable changes in the direction of growing concentration, though, quite clearly they were not enough to produce gains in productivity; indeed quite the reverse occurred.

The second section of this survey dealt with the general pattern of productivity in the inter-war period; in relation to that, the aim of this section has been to illustrate in a little more detail some of the reasons behind that pattern. One conclusion is most apparent from the available evidence : the absence of any kind of clear statistical distinction between 'old' and 'new' industries is correspondingly borne out in terms of business organisation and methods.

56

5 The Balance of Payments

FLUCTUATIONS in external trade were clearly an active element in the cyclical downswings of the early part of the period, but thereafter the relative stagnation of British trade can be regarded as more of a long-term drag on the economy. The statistics of trade which were available in the inter-war period, and which have been used directly by some earlier historians, contain a number of inaccuracies. Since then there has been a great deal of reworking of the figures by a number of experts, and the pattern of British trade is now fairly clear.

Table 5

Volume of U.K. Imports and Exports, 1919–38

(1913 = 100)

	Imports	Exports		Imports	Exports
1919	87·7	54·9	1929	114·8	81·3
1920	87·7	70·3	1930	111·1	65·9
1921	74·1	49·5	1931	113·6	50·5
1922	85·2	68·1	1932	98·8	50·5
1923	92·6	74·7	1933	98·8	51·6
1924	103·7	75·8	1934	103·7	54·9
1925	107·4	74·7	1935	104·9	59·3
1926	109·9	67·0	1936	112·3	59·3
1927	112·3	76·9	1937	118·5	64·8
1928	108·6	79·1	1938	113·6	57·1

Source: London and Cambridge Economic Service (1967, Table K).

During the 1920s, British trade, by comparison with that of other large trading nations, was neither sufficently competitive nor concentrated in the growth sectors of international trade; and the negative effects of this on the trade balance were not neutralised by income, price or terms of trade effects. Recent research by Maizels (1963) indicates, however, that the composition of British exports became a less important factor during the 1930s. Then, the predominant influences were the general slump in world trade and the limited export market for more complex manufactured goods. Moreover, these trends simply emphasise the point, which has already been made, of the need for changes in the shape of the economy with the consequently declining proportionate role of trade within it – a fact which a report of the twenties was to some extent aware of.[19] Two factors underlay this need: as an advanced economy such as Great Britain became better off, it necessarily tended to spend a declining proportion of its income on basic commodities such as food, which were largely imported from abroad; and the nature of technological change not only produced demands for quite new raw materials, but it also involved more complicated methods of combining given amounts of raw materials so that the demand of industrial countries for such materials did not rise in proportion to the value of final goods produced. Together these factors resulted in a proportionate drop in income generated in other countries by Britain's demand for imports, and this consequently led to a proportionate fall in the demand for British exports and hence a declining proportionate role for foreign trade in the generation of British national income. Moreover, at the time this could not, to any significant extent, be compensated for by growing trade in manufactured goods between advanced economies such as has emerged since the Second World War.

Another general consequence of these developments has been strikingly evident since the Second World War, though it had its origins in the inter-war period. The international trading community was beginning to split into groups in a way which resulted in a large share of the most profitable international trade becoming the preserve of the advanced economies – a process fostered by the establishment of what are, ostensibly, international trading organisations. It is true, nevertheless, that the failure to develop such organisations, particularly in the 1930s, was a factor

[19] See Balfour Commitee (Committee on Industry and Trade), *Survey of Overseas Markets* (1925) pp. 6–26.

hampering British trade in common with that of other advanced economies. Conversely, it seems clear that, during the period, trade could no longer function as an engine of growth for emerging economies;[20] and Britain, which had traditionally operated this engine, had to adjust its trading pattern accordingly.

In real terms British domestic exports never achieved their 1913 level between the wars; and even in money terms they remained considerably below the 1913 level between 1931 and 1939. British exports fared worse than world trade over the period as a whole, especially in the 1920s. The major sources of this decline are to be found in the catastrophic falls in the exports of cotton yarn and piece goods, and coal. Yet, of domestic exports in terms of value, in 1937 coal still accounted for 8 per cent, cotton goods 13 per cent, iron and steel 9·5 per cent and woollen goods 5·9 per cent, as against 4·7 per cent for vehicles and aircraft, 2·4 per cent for electrical goods and 4·7 per cent for chemicals. Associated with these trends were shifts in distribution : broadly this led to declines in exports to India, Asiatic markets generally, South America, Europe and the United States, and a rise in exports to the Empire countries as a whole, so that by the end of the period they were accounting for nearly 50 per cent of the total; this latter trend was a particular feature of the 1930s. Imports, by contrast, were generally above the pre-war level during the inter-war years. The main reasons for this were that a large proportion of imports – foodstuffs and raw materials – were in fairly inelastic demand, the terms of trade were strongly in Britain's favour taking the period as a whole, and a larger share of its total overseas earnings was used to buy overseas imports instead of, as before the war, going to provide for new foreign investment. At the same time, however, there were some sharp rises in imports of manufactured goods at certain points during the period. Moreover, in association with the changing distribu-

[20] Such countries could not generate domestic income by being able to offer substantial price reductions on a narrow range of primary, or simple manufactured, goods, traded in the international market. See Wicksell Lectures 1953–1964, *International Trade and Finance* (Stockholm, 1965) pp. 45–94; A. K. Cairncross, *Factors in Economic Development* (1962) part III.

tion of exports, the whole pattern of multilateral settlement of debts, on which the British position had rested before 1913, was seriously undermined; the most striking example of this was the shrinking in the surplus with India which had been used to settle something like one-half of British trade debts. And finally, against the trends for exports, British imports rose as a proportion of world imports: from approximately 15 per cent in 1913 to approximately 17 per cent by 1937.

In the 1920s world trade continued to grow and therefore, in this respect, Britain undoubtedly fared worse than the international economy as a whole. Unfortunately, not enough is known about the price elasticity of demand for British exports, but it has already been suggested in Section 3 above that the competitive position would have been little affected if Britain had returned to gold at a 10·0 per cent devaluation on the pre-war level. In addition, many commentators have drawn attention to the income effect of continuously falling primary product prices on countries taking British exports – and it must be borne in mind that in 1913 40·0 per cent of British manufactured exports had gone to semi-industrial markets. Furthermore, such was the nature of competition that the probability of downward adjustments of prices by competitors, particularly in Asia, was very great. Eastern industrialisation was not merely a war-time phenomenon: it had a longer pedigree. Japan, in particular, showed itself determined to use all manner of protective devices to ensure the continued growth of its economy.

More fundamentally, the causes of Britain's declining trade position would appear to have been structural maladjustments in international trade, which were associated with the declining trade in staple goods and the relatively low levels of trade in more advanced manufactured goods. And even allowing for tariffs, the price-competitive argument loses much of its force when one observes the continuing deterioration in British trade in the 1930s when the gold standard was no longer in operation.

There is general acceptance of the view that there is more excuse for Britain's dismal trade performance in the 1930s than in the 1920s, because of the general collapse in the international economy. Even so, tariff protection and licensing systems were

60

developing in the 1920s and the political settlement of Versailles doubled the number of independent customs administrations in Central and Eastern Europe. But eventually Britain itself was forced to run for protection in 1931. This was a major political issue, and was seen by certain sections of the Conservative Party as the final triumph and justification of the movement started by Joseph Chamberlain before the war. In terms of its effects on British economic development, however, commentators are generally agreed that it was of minor importance. Yet there is the nagging question, which is probably unanswerable, as to what extent the return to protection did provide a certain amount of insulation to industry in the form of reducing the pressure upon it to adapt more to international trading conditions; and whether such an attitude was reinforced by the favourable turn in demand which sprang from the domestic rearmament programme in the 1930s. Furthermore, the greater efficiency of foreign producers of such goods as motor vehicles, rayon and certain electrical goods emphasises the question concerning the protective nature of tariffs. Among the staple industries, the iron and steel industry is a well-documented – and indeed a most important – example of lagging efficiency of British producers as against major foreign competitors; but it operated behind a tariff wall.

Finally, on the visible trade side of the external account brief mention should be made of the importance of the 'new' industries or, more accurately, new products. It has already been indicated that the leading examples of these formed a small part of exports. Certainly there is no reason to argue that, in the trading conditions of the 1930s, they could have achieved a great deal more. But when one reflects on the pattern of trade in sophisticated manufactures of the 'new' goods type that has emerged since the Second World War, and on the relationship between this and long-term economic growth, then one becomes aware that there was a distinct limit to the level of economic growth, or 'recovery', that was possible in the 1930s.[21] Putting it another way, one can ask to what extent the British economy was hampered by a discontinuity in international economic development, particularly

[21] See Postan, *Economic History of Western Europe*, chap. 4.

as it affected the advanced nations: a discontinuity that could not be overcome until there was a return to fuller international economic relations and, indeed, recovery in the other major economies. In turn, this raises the question of the relationship between trade and growth. While there is current disagreement among economists as to the precise nature of this relationship, the argument is largely concerned with development since the Second World War and is thus an argument about margins at a high level of trade; by contrast, the distinguishing feature of the inter-war period is the low absolute level of trade, and there seems no reason to doubt that this had a directly depressing effect on growth.

The overall balance of payments position is shown in Table 6 opposite. In comparison with the pre-war period, Britain no longer generated a large enough surplus on invisible and overseas investment accounts to plug the negative trade balance and to provide a large and growing surplus for further foreign investment. In part this resulted from the liquidation of some overseas investments during and after the war, but mainly from falling income. In addition, during the period there were both indirect and direct controls on overseas lending; and such factors as international insecurity and the decline of foreign flotations in London reduced the incentive among British investors to invest abroad.

Once again, it has been suggested by Moggridge (1969) that invisible earnings in the 1920s, particularly from shipping, might have benefited directly from a devalued pound. But quite apart from the fact that those earnings dropped even more spectacularly in the 1930s, it was by no means an issue of price competitiveness in this sphere: London was no longer strong enough to perform its pre-1914 financial role; Britain's shipping services became plainly inferior through lack of innovation; British trade was no longer dominant enough to give Britain an advantage in the provision of financial services; and low interest rates in the thirties enabled foreigners to convert their borrowings in London and thus reduce the country's income from these sources.

The various figures in Table 6 have to be interpreted with extreme care since their accuracy is far from beyond reproach; it

62

Table 6

U.K. Balance of Payments, 1919–38
($£$ million)

	Trade balance (valued f.o.b.)	Net income invisibles	Current account balance	Net long-term capital movements	Overall balance*
1919	−501	372	−129	n.a.	n.a.
1920	−180	415	235	n.a.	n.a.
1921	−165	284	119	n.a.	n.a.
1922	−77	250	173	n.a.	n.a.
1923	−98	267	169	n.a.	n.a.
1924	−211	252	41	−134	−93
1925	−259	306	47	−88	−41
1926	−339	324	−15	−85	−100
1927	−265	347	82	−105	−23
1928	−233	356	123	−108	15
1929	−259	362	103	−47	56
1930	−282	310	28	−19	9
1931	−323	218	−105	1	−104
1932	−217	166	−51	21	−30
1933	−196	196	0	--6	−6
1934	−221	214	−7	−36	−43
1935	−185	217	32	−40	−8
1936	−260	243	−17	26	9
1937	−339	283	−56	11	−45
1938	−284	230	−54	40	−14

* i.e. excluding gold and short-term capital movements.

Sources: London and Cambridge Economic Service (1967, Table N, with minor corrections); Kahn (1946, 126).

is most unwise to place any heavy reliance on them. Furthermore, precise figures for total British overseas investment at the end of the period are not available; the best estimate would suggest that they were worth £3,700 million, which was some 7 per cent lower than in 1913, in money terms. In the 1920s the supply of long-term international capital had been distorted by the artificial currents of reparations payments; and with the collapse of international confidence in the 1930s capital flows were cut to very low levels. Generally, the failure to restore an international capital market was to some extent a limiting factor on Britain's and other countries' economic growth. But in any event Britain would necessarily have to play a far less prominent role in this field in the future than it had done in the past.

Finally, there were substantial gold and short-term capital movements during the 1930s. These were not overall balancing items in origin, but rather they reflected the comparative safety of London as against other financial centres as a depository for gold and currency reserves. At the same time these large movements did not have any effects on the domestic economy because they were insulated from it through the operation of the Exchange Equalisation Account. It is important to recognise the true nature of these flows, however, when interpreting balance of payments figures for this period.

6 Aspects of Economic Thought and Policy

IT is possible to argue that shortcomings in this field constitute the most important factor in limiting growth of the economy between 1918 and 1939. Certain aspects of policy have already been considered. But before other areas are reviewed, it is as well to draw attention to the scale of the Government's indirect effect on the economy. Even in the pre-war period U.K. public expenditure (central and local) average 12 per cent of gross national product, and this made the Government by far the largest economic institution in the country. Over the war period itself, the proportion increased to one-half, though during the twenties and thirties it dropped back to an average of between 24 per cent and 29 per cent, with a sharp rise to nearly 35 per cent over the rearmament period of 1938–9. It is necessary to qualify this, however, by the fact that in 1929 about one-quarter of public expenditure was accounted for by interest payments on the national debt, as compared with 6 per cent in 1913. And the official attitude towards income and expenditure was dominated by the Treasury's Gladstonian view that the reduction of the national debt was the primary task of public finance. Direct expenditure on goods and services by public authorities averaged between 12 per cent and 16 per cent of gross national product between 1920 and 1937, with a sharp rise to 20 per cent in 1938.

The main question in the realm of public finance for these years is the net effect on the economy of budgetary policy. The general aim was to balance the budget, though the period as a whole was one of budget surpluses (usually proportionately small). In only one year, 1932–3, was there a deficit (a mere £6 million), and only in 1938–9 was an almost exact balance achieved. It is unwise, however, to deduce much from these figures : the statistics are impossible to evaluate with any precision because so little is known about the budgetary and accounting procedures employed by the Exchequer during those years; and even if there were much more disaggregated data, it would be necessary to do a sophisticated econometric analysis of government income and expenditure before it would be possible to make any judgements on the overall, net effect of budgetary policy. Clearly, even a balanced budget can have expansionary effects if it involves the transfer of money between groups in such a way as to raise the average propensity to consume. To some extent, therefore, in this way a budget multiplier might have operated within the policy which has been described. But given the size of budgets and the absence of substantial deficits, in terms of possible alternatives the policy which was followed could in no way be described as expansionary. If one had to make an informed guess as to the actual effects, one would reckon that, taking the period as a whole, budgets were fairly neutral – and in the conditions of the period this is as good as saying that the overall effect was contractionary.

Neutral budgets were, however, the product of far from neutral judgements on the nature and limits of government expenditure. The May Report has already been cited in relation to financial policy, but it was also taken by the authorities as providing the authoritative answer to what was generally regarded as the apostasy of the Macmillan Report. It was in vain that the Minority Report of the May Committee, written by its trade union members, drew attention to the abandonment of truths and values which action in support of the majority's recommendations would necessarily entail : 'Public expenditure has ample justification when it rests primarily on the necessity for readjusting the use of national income in such a manner as to transfer expenditure from less essential or desirable channels into those which are designed to mitigate social injustices, or those which improve the economic structure of the nation' (May Committee, 1931, 229).

Many writers have characterised the nature of government economic policy as *ad hoc* and lacking in understanding of the fundamental causes of the problems with which it sought to deal. The general manner in which the trend of long-term economic development increased the need for more central direction of the economy has been pointed out by Ashworth (1966) in relation to the late Victorian period. Furthermore, the dislocations and aftermath of the First World War made reliance on a largely self-regulating economy entirely misplaced. For fairly obvious historical reasons, major government involvement in the economy first centred on financial policy. This has already been discussed in some detail, but two further points should be mentioned here. First, as a number of economic historians have shown, successive governments took the view that they had ultimate responsibility for restoring sound finance, since this provided the framework within which all other economic activity took place. And secondly, such a view demonstrated the very severe limitations which governments imposed on their own actions in economic affairs. This is perhaps best illustrated by MacDonald and Snowden, who must be credited as the leading representatives of a political philosophy based on the essential truth of the need for central control of the very basis of the economy, but who regarded decisions about the financial system as being almost beyond politics. If classical orthodoxy had thus captured the leadership of the Labour Party, the accepted limits to independent government action are clear enough. In the 1930s, as has been observed, the Government was able to retire from active consideration of financial matters, since pressures at this point had been substantially relieved by the turn in international financial conditions.

Another major area of government policy, or lack of it, was unemployment. Hancock (1962) has analysed the various measures which go under the name of employment policy, and certain general features are all too obvious. Legislation was introduced in an *ad hoc* manner and showed little understanding of the basic causes of the problem. At the level of public debate, Gilbert (1970, 306–7) has given some indication of the importance attached to the subject as late as 1934, when there were still over one million unemployed : a complex Unemployment Bill was introduced in that year, yet more days of parliamentary time were given to the India Bill, which also took up more columns of newsprint and was by far the more popular subject for debate within the Conservative Party.

At the same time, however, it is possible to argue that government attitudes on this central issue were not far behind 'best informed' opinion on the subject. There was, as one might expect, a fundamentalist approach to the matter, which attributed unemployment to failings in human character, but it is probably true to say that Beveridge, particularly through his book *Unemployment: A Problem of Industry* (1909), still represented the most effective body of analysis on the issue. Yet this analysis was not rooted in a clear economic understanding of the problem. Beveridge saw unemployment as a result of frictions in the labour market, the effects of which could be eased and overcome through insurance and labour exchanges. For him the function of government was, therefore, to establish the necessary administrative machinery to achieve this. In 1934, for example, Beveridge revealed his attitude to unemployment insurance when 'one of [his] proudest boasts was that, under the aegis of his committee [the Unemployment Insurance Statutory Committee], contributors had repaid all previous borrowings from the Treasury. Even book-keeping transactions, it would seem, could be represented as policy triumphs' (cited by Winch, 1969, 211). On the general question of depression Beveridge believed, with Pigou, that cuts in wages would provide an important part of the solution. Moreover, the continued, and ostensibly 'efficient', operation of Friendly Societies strengthened official belief in the self-financing insurance principle. Although the Unemployment Assistance Board, established in 1934, was a big step forward in rationalising the whole system of unemployment relief, it did not operate satisfactorily until the very end of the period; not least because of the problem of fixing relief rates which were not above the low wages paid in certain sectors of industry.

Unemployment policy was part of the wider issue of government planning. Planning became a vogue subject in the 1930s, though the beginnings of wide interest in this might be dated by the publication of the Liberal Party's *Britain's Industrial Future* (1928). It was, too, an integral part of the famous 'Mosley Principles' of 1930.[22] Nevertheless, some political and social historians confuse planning with the Keynesian approach to economic stability. The latter is concerned with short-term

[22] Sir Oswald Mosley, who, at the time, was a leading member of the Labour Party, drew up an impressive programme of action to deal with unemployment.

équilibrium and the full employment of resources, whereas the former is directed primarily towards devising means of effecting longer-term structural adjustments in order to achieve what is considered to be a satisfactory level of economic growth. It can be suggested that such leading economists as Robertson and Pigou were perhaps nearer the mark than Keynes on the issue of planing.[23] It is, in any event, a subject worthy of much fuller investigation. In addition, the Macmillan Report also spent a great deal of time with much insight in discussing aspects of planning. Unfortunately, some of the most important of its recommendations were not unanimously supported, and the case for much more direct government involvement in industry was left to be put in as an addendum to the main Report (1931, 203–9).

Furthermore, there is some confusion among recent writers over the achievements in the field of 'planning' during the 1930s. Beer, for example, states : 'Government decisions in these years endowed Britain with a pattern of economic policy that was comprehensive and radically different from that of previous generations.'[24] This view relates particularly to 'industrial reorganisation policies' of the period. But anyone who cares to read through one of the many descriptive accounts of various schemes which were introduced cannot but fail to be impressed by the fact that the one thing they have in common is that they were *ad hoc* and somewhat unrelated responses to immediate difficulties. Little more than that !

The Government's main effort in industrial planning was the Special Areas policy introduced in 1934, but there is virtually unanimous agreement among commentators that it was quite inadequate and failed to deal with the fundamental causes of the problem of depressed areas. Indeed, the Special Areas Commissioner for England and Wales experienced so much obstruction from the Government that he eventually resigned. Yet the charge that this policy was little more than a weak palliative, and that it did not treat the localisation of unemployment as part of the general problem of economic growth, could be levelled at much

[23] See, for example, Youngson (1967, 269 ff.), for an introduction to this question.
[24] See S. H. Beer, *Modern British Politics* (1965) p. 279.

more recent exercises in this field. Somewhat later the Government set up a Royal Commission on the Distribution of the Industrial Population (the Barlow Commission) which produced its final report in 1940. Setting up this inquiry was at least a recognition that industrial location was a matter for serious analysis and discussion, and the Barlow Commission collected a great deal of evidence on the subject. It also showed some awareness of the general costs of the pattern of development that was occurring, though it did not analyse this in any depth, since it was hampered by the lack of crucial evidence on costs. It recommended, however, that the Government should adopt a more positive role by taking stronger powers for regulating industrial development.

One area, deserving special mention, in which the Government was quite active, though not particularly effective, was that of transport. Here the need for clear direction was great and the opportunities for achieving noticeable improvement considerable. For example, in the case of road transport there was obviously a splendid opportunity for combining sound planning with public works expenditure to relieve unemployment. But the opportunity was lost; and after 1930 new main-road building virtually came to an end. The railways were weakened by the long-term effects of changes in the composition of their traffic and competition from motor vehicles, and afflicted by the shorter-term consequences of the depression. Yet official thinking on railways advanced little beyond the traditional nineteenth-century concern over a railway monopoly; moreover, for all its shortcomings, earlier policy could at least claim to have been more determined by general principles. The Railway Act of 1921, which laid the foundation of inter-war railway policy, has been described as a grand compromise and the product of the desire for administrative tidiness. And although a recent study (Aldcroft, 1968) alleges that, generally, railway companies were unenterprising in their pricing policies and that their accounting procedures were far from adequate enough to give them a precise measure of their costs of operation, nevertheless throughout the period they were largely discouraged from becoming more enterprising by the many restrictions which the Government imposed upon them.

70

Even more serious was the failure to integrate road and rail policy – quite apart from the absence of any analysis of the much larger and complex relationship between this and urban planning. The only area of transport in which the Government did take a more positive role, because, eventually, there was no alternative, was civil aviation. The setting up of B.O.A.C. in 1939 was a major change of policy from what had gone before when the Government had been content to act in this area through the Imperial Airways Company, as its so-called 'chosen instrument', and in this way avoid any direct responsibility for putting civil aviation on a sound economic footing.

This latter development is illustrative of a wider one; the growth of public corporations. The B.B.C. and the Central Electricity Generating Board are two outstanding examples. But, as Mowat (1955, 342) had observed, the establishment of these corporations was the result of *force majeure* and in no sense represented a general strategy. In the case of the B.B.C., official thinking was much influenced by the apparent chaos in broadcasting in the United States, which had arisen from the existence of a number of rival stations.

More generally, practically all aspects of sound economic policy had, necessarily, to be based on adequate statistical information. Comprehensive economic statistics are of fairly recent origin and our present discussion of the period has frequently been hampered for want of reliable data of this kind. Moreover, much of the material which we have been able to draw on has been constructed only in recent years. However, the lack of such data did not go unnoticed at the time. The Balfour Committee (1928, 33–5) emphasised the need for such information and criticised the fact that in the official zest for economy a number of extremely useful statistical agencies which had been started during the war had been subsequently closed down. In part, too, this lack reflected the machinery of government which in its existing form was not adapted to the kind of functions which we have been discussing. Quite apart from the dominance of the Treasury (which appears to have developed into a long-standing tradition of British government) and the relatively low status of the ministries or departments responsible for economic and social matters, the training of senior civil servants was largely unrelated to the tasks that they might have been expected to perform.

Economic thought and its relationship to policy is another facet to be considered. Winch (1969) has provided a clear and interesting analysis of this subject, though it is cast a little too rigidly in a Keynesian mould. The most obvious point to emerge, however, is the disagreement between economists during the inter-war period. This has also been illustrated by Hancock (1960) in the context of the 1920s. As a characteristic of economists it is not, of course, peculiar to the inter-war years, since any impartial observer is aware that it is just as pronounced in present-day discussions of economic problems in the real world. But in the 1920s and 1930s the consequences were more serious than they are today. At the expense of oversimplifying the contrast, one might say that the debate then was on whether the Government could, or indeed should, make a major contribution towards attempting to maintain a high level of economic prosperity, whereas today the crucial nature of this role is an accepted fact – among all but a few economic eccentrics – and the argument is about alternative methods of achieving this.

In the matter of major issues which arose during the period, Winch seeks to defend Keynes's consistency, though he subsequently provides ample evidence of the manner in which Keynes frequently changed his mind. Keynes himself admitted that his views had undergone considerable changes: 'The relation between this book [*The General Theory of Employment, Interest and Money*] and my *Treatise on Money*, which I published five years ago, is probably clearer to myself than it will be to others; what in my own mind is a natural evolution in a line of thought which I have been pursuing for several years, may strike the reader as a confusing change of view.'[25] Furthermore, as has been suggested earlier, Keynes's method of conducting debates was not always calculated to win friends and influence people. Moreover, the link between economic theory and economic policy was a very tenuous one. The Government preferred to be guided by 'conven-

[25] John Maynard Keynes, *The General Theory of Employment, Interest and Money* 1954 ed.) p. vi.

tional wisdom'; and in so far as the views of such economists as Cannan, Gregory, Hawtrey, Hayek, Pigou and Robbins accorded with this they found favour in official circles. There were, too, alternative views for the Government to absorb, including quite primitive notions such as the 'Capital Fund Theory' which argued that government expenditure in support of public works would simply be taking capital from other uses and would thus be 'borrowing from future growth' – a theory which was eagerly adopted by the Treasury. It is perhaps worth noting that the *General Theory* was not published until 1936, and the form of its presentation can be regarded as much as an essay in persuasion as a comprehensive analysis of the short-term equilibrium of the economy.

Thus the backwardness of government policy in many aspects of economic development must be counted as a central weakness throughout this period. There was, it is true, a noticeable increase in government economic activity in the 1930s, but in no way did it amount to a managed economy, in the modern sense of the term. In the last analysis, however, the issue was one of fundamental political philosophy, and it therefore has to be seen in the broader context of political history. Thus, although ostensibly the radicalism of the Liberal Party was supplanted by the more thoroughgoing socialism of the Labour Party, in practice it made very little difference to the operation of government. The determination of MacDonald to establish Labour as a party fit to govern, and the genuine preference of his leading associates for traditional rather than truly socialist programmes of action, contributed to the consensus in support of orthodoxy – a consensus which at times was elevated into a doctrine of 'the national interest'. Changes in the direction of more governmental control of economic and social matters did occur, though not as a result of dramatic conversion or clear understanding of the nature of the economy. They developed through a process of reluctant pragmatism, in which new principles emerged only slowly. Unfortunately, the main burden of this slow change was thrown on to those least able to bear it.

7 Labour

UNEMPLOYMENT levels have to be seen against the background of a substantial rise in the labour force between 1918 and 1939 : the number of insured employees rose from 11·5 million in 1923 to nearly 16 million by 1939. It must be emphasised, however, that figures for the total labour force are subject to some significant margin of error. Estimates have to be made, since not all workers were insured and it is practically impossible to calculate what proportion of women can be counted as part of the labour force. Nevertheless, in broad terms, the increase resulted from a steady fall in the death rate so that the average age of the population and of the labour force was rising. This conjunction of factors led to a great deal of concern in some quarters because of fears of an eventual decline in total population with the consequent burden of an increasing proportion of retired people. Although these fears were not realised, the nature of the change in the population and the labour force did have immediate economic effects. It exacerbated the unemployment problem and reduced the level of occupational and geographical mobility.

The figures for internal migration are far from complete and difficult to interpret. Nevertheless, those data that are available do illustrate a broad movement from the less prosperous to the more prosperous regions of the country, in particular a movement to the South-east. Against this, however, the absolute numbers were not high, and in proportionate terms they do not appear to have had a major impact. Levels of unemployment in the depressed areas were not materially affected by migration, and movements within properous areas and within depressed areas sometimes outweighed flows between the two different types of region. Probably the main migration movement was from city centres to new suburbs, in the more prosperous areas.

The nature of the depressed regions has already been commented on. For the period 1932–7 the rate of unemployment in London and the South-east region was 9·3 per cent as compared with 20·5 per cent for Scotland and 30·9 per cent for Wales. Correspondingly, there were variations between industries. In 1932 the range was from 62·0 per cent in shipbuilding and repairing to 5·9 per cent in tramway and omnibus services. Even as late as 1937 the contrasting pattern was still very evident. As a percentage of the mean rate of unemployment for the United Kingdom, the range varied all the way from 57·0 per cent for the Midlands, 58·0 per cent for the South-east and 79·0 per cent for London, to 146·0 per cent for Scotland, 183·0 per cent for the North and 233·0 per cent for Wales. For individual industries the actual rate still varied from 3·1 per cent to 27·5 per cent. In short, despite the upswing in the economy in the 1930s, the reduction of unemployment was uneven and far from complete. Indeed, 'in three of the four prosperous regions (London, the South-east, and the South-west) the unemployment rate in 1937 was still higher than in 1929'; and overall, 'only in the Midlands and North Eastern divisions were the unemployment rates of 1937 lower than in 1929' (Richardson, 1967, 273). In part, of course, some of this unemployment was irreducible; for example when rearmament led to the recovery of the iron and steel industry in certain depressed areas, labour shortages appeared despite the continued existence of unemployment. The reason was largely one of older men being out of work for so long that they had become, in effect, unemployable. But this represented economic and social waste for all that.

While unemployment data are open to relatively clear interpretaton, the same cannot be said of data relating to wages and earnings. There is, of course, the perennial problem of relating wages to earnings, which is bound up with the level of unemployment and with the difficulty of making allowance for such factors as differentials, regional variations and the income of the family group. And in so many cases data just do not exist. Moreover, while the brief summary which follows is limited to wages, it is important to note that over the period as a whole occupational mobility was reducing the size of the wage-earning group, and this is therefore a concealed element making for more prosperity than is at first apparent.

Most of the available figures have recently been brought together by Phelps Brown and Browne (1968) in an inter-country study of wages. But for those wishing to delve deeper, the most comprehensive information is contained in the earlier study by Chapman and Knight (1953). Certain general conclusions emerge but, it is necessary to repeat, they do cover quite diverse patterns underneath. For those who remained in employment, there was a steady but not spectacular rise in real wages; an increase of some 18 per cent between 1920 and 1938. In general terms, it was mainly the product of fairly constant money wages combined with a favourable downward movement in average prices. The biggest individual rises were registered by agriculture and forestry, fishing, printing, utilities, transport and communications, distributive trades and local government service; whilst the lowest were shown by mining and quarrying, iron and steel, shipbuilding and construction, textile industries and professional services. In the light of what is known of some of these industries it is immediately clear that these changes have to be interpreted carefully. Due attention has to be paid to the comparative levels of wages in different groups at the beginning of the period; for example, in relation to other industries agricultural wages were comparatively so low in 1920 that despite a 38 per cent increase by 1938 they were still among the lowest of all industrial groups. Furthermore, allowance has to be made for reductions in hours of work and the provision of holidays. Unfortunately, there is not space to consider this, but it is worth noting that some 11 million out of 20 million workers were entitled to holidays with pay by 1939, though most of the gain which this represented was made in the last two years or so of the period.

Some econometric analyses have hypothesised a relationship between the course of wages and the level of unemployment; but although the studies of Phillips (1958) and Lipsey (1960) indicate some inverse correlation between the two variables, the overall pattern is undoubtedly determined by a much wider variety of factors. Indeed, Phelps Brown and Browne (1968, 221–34, 319–22) have pointed out that on the basis of evidence from a number of countries the hypothesis does not hold good: such factors as general price structure, the level of profits and external competitiveness also play an active part in wage determination. And it is by no means self-evident that an increase in unemployment implies an equal and proportionate reduction in union bargaining power. Furthermore, in this connection attention can be drawn to a familiar contemporary argument, which has been repeated by some later commentators, that the stickiness of wages downwards raised unemployment by keeping costs at a level that prevented the growth of sales and by restricting occupational mobility. But this argument misses the point that in the inter-war years lower wages would have intensified the deficiency of demand which was a major cause of unemployment while, as has been shown, the nature and extent of occupational mobility was part of the complex of problems affecting industrial structure and the distribution of unemployment; and throughout the period there was certainly no overall potential shortage of labour.

At another level, Richardson (1962, 1967), as has been noted, sees increased real wages in the early thirties as an important connecting link between cyclical upswing and structural change: increasing real wages led to growing demands for the products of the so-called new industries. Even in the absence of more detailed information, there seems to be no reason for doubting this link, but the more relevant point is that it was no more than a secondary compensatory factor against the larger effects of the depression; in other words, had there been a consistently higher growth rate than was achieved, and no depression, total real income would have been even higher and demands for new goods would have arisen sooner and would have grown more rapidly. Indeed, the sales figures for many new consumer durables, at the very end of the period, show clearly that these goods were mainly the prerogative of the middle and upper classes.

It is doubtful whether labour's gain in terms of real wages was matched in terms of the total distribution of income. Here the evidence is even less comprehensive, but the studies of A. L.

77

Bowley (1937), Barna (1945), Clark (1951) and others show fairly convincingly that the magnitudes are of such an order as to suggest that there was little absolute change in shares even if there was some noticeable proportionate change during the 1930s.[26] The share of gross national income going to wage-earners actually *fell* from 39·4 per cent in 1920–9 to 39·0 per cent in 1930–9; conversely, salaries rose from 17·6 per cent to 20·2 per cent. Total employment incomes rose only slightly, from 59·7 per cent to 61·0 per cent of all income. However, this has to be balanced by the fact, noticed above, that the proportionate size of the wage-labour force was declining. So far as transfer payments were concerned, they became larger in the thirties than in the twenties, but even by the end of the period a high proportion of payments was made within the wage-earning group – not least, of course, because of the operation of the insurance principle in major areas of social welfare. And some commentators, such as Hicks (op. cit.) and Mowat (1955, pp. 490 ff.), judge the redistributive effects of the social services to have been quite small.

Whether taxation became more progressive or not, is equally difficult to be precise about. Income tax rose, but the pattern of indirect taxation as it affected different sections of wage-earners is not clear. Certainly, some of the contemporary surveys on diet could be taken as suggesting that the regressive effects of indirect taxation were quite sharp at low levels of income. Finally, in absolute terms, there was little effective taxation of wealth. From the available evidence, therefore, it does not appear that the wealthier classes were unduly penalised during these years, even though in proportionate terms their tax burden was increasing.

Although it is not possible to distinguish any direct relationship between unionisation and wages, it is nevertheless true, of course, that the whole development of industrial relations has a big bearing on economic performance. Again, it has to be said that a great deal more research needs to be done in this field. There is, it is true, a substantial literature on individual unions and union

[26] See also J. R. Hicks, *The Social Framework* (Oxford, 1942) esp. pp. 179–91; and G. F. Shirras and L. Rostas, *The Burden of British Taxation* (1942).

leaders, but it is of very uneven quality. Indeed, the most useful study is Bullock's (1960) biography of Bevin, since it contains many insights into the broader aspects of union development during this period. Many writers have commented on the improving relations between employers and unions at the national level, which can be seen, for example, in the Mond–Turner talks at the end of the twenties. Trade union leaders were gradually learning to express their views collectively on national issues – particularly through the T.U.C. – and thereby to increase their general influence; while the acceptance by the Government of the need to include union representatives on investigations which touched directly on union interests is proof of the national role which they had come to play. Furthermore, in the process many labour leaders abandoned the doctrines of Marx for a somewhat more practical approach to economic affairs.

Yet at the lower level of individual unions and individual firms, the indications are that industrial relations were developing slowly and, because of this, they exerted another drag on the overall growth of the economy. On the management side there was insufficient understanding of the crucial link between efficiency and good labour relations; and, perhaps more important, evidence of this can be found among the newest sectors of industry, thus providing yet another reason for doubting the 'old–new' dichotomy. On the union side there was unwillingness to surrender old methods of training and traditional forms of demarcation. These shortcomings were probably most acute in the staple industries, which required the greatest degree of change; though in these cases they can perhaps be explained in terms of defensive reactions in the absence of adequate provision for redundancy and unemployment. But the same cannot be said of rapidly developing industries such as those of motor vehicles and artificial fibres; yet all too frequently the same pattern of fragmented union structure, which made negotiations between management and unions difficult and likely to lead to ill feeling and inefficiency, was repeated.

8 Depression and Recovery

IN making a general appraisal of the inter-war period, one is immediately up against the methodological problem of evaluating the economic effects of the First World War; and unless one is prepared to contemplate the kind of heroic assumptions made in some studies in econometric history, which might require the assumption that the war did not occur, the question is to some extent unanswerable. This subject has, moreover, been discussed in some detail by Milward (1970). But a few comments in relation to the theme of the present study seem to be in order. Quite clearly there were fairly immediate consequences from the war in terms of inflation and the subsequent depression. There were, too, more persistent effects such as the collapse of the international financial system, the breakdown of normal international capital movements, and the disrupting effects of reparations payments. The best account of these events is probably still that given in Keynes's brilliant essay *The Economic Consequences of the Peace* (1919). Against this, if one takes a broader view, the effect of the war appears to have been predominantly one of exacerbating already existing weaknesses in the British economy; though the work of Ashworth (1960, 1966) and Saul (1960) suggests that these weaknesses were not pronounced before 1914 and were probably a feature of the Edwardian, rather than of the late Victorian, economy.

A dominant feature of the 1920s, however, was the strong determination to get back to the pre-war situation, even though in terms of sound policy it was the reverse of what was required. The war provided an easy rationalisation for current ills. Indeed, although many writers claim that the upheaval of war produced big social changes, it is perhaps not unreasonable to treat this with some reserve in the light of subsequent economic policies and of the evidence of the apparently easy conscience with which such promises as 'Homes fit for heroes' were blatantly broken. In total, however, the evidence which has been reviewed on various aspects of the economy strongly supports the argument that the war was a secondary factor in determining economic development between 1918 and 1939.

More generally, this review has concentrated on the central issue of the growth performance of the economy, while at the same time attention has been drawn to the pronounced cyclical swings in the level of activity. But it has been observed that the relaionship between these two elements is exceedingly complex and impossible to disentangle. For this reason, to talk of depression and recovery in the inter-war period carries with it the danger of confusion – a confusion analogous to that of failing to distinguish between movements along demand or supply curves, with upward or downward shifts in such curves. This is particularly the case with what is frequently regarded as the 'recovery of the thirties'. The real issue, which has already been critically discussed, is whether the upswing from 1932–3 onwards was just a recovery in a cyclical sense, or whether it incorporated a shift to a higher trend of economic growth.

The outstanding fact is that the cyclical upswing persisted until 1937 when there was a sharp downswing; and the nature of the downswing illustrates the limited basis to growth in the previous period. Furthermore, the succeeding upturn in activity was based on the older sectors of industry. There were thus periods of cyclical depression and recovery, but the statistical evidence does not support the view that within these phases the economy moved on to a higher growth plane. In the growth sense, therefore, it is difficult to see how one can speak of 'recovery' in the inter-war years. There was not recovery in the sense that there was a return in the 1930s to previously high levels of growth, since growth was faily constant over the whole period; there was not recovery in the sense that the health of the economy improved so much over the 1930s as to make it unrecognisable from its previous state.

Some economic historians have drawn international comparisons of economic growth which reflect favourably on the

British economy during the inter-war years; yet this does not seem to be a meaningful exercise. For one thing, it is virtually impossible to test whether the various statistics that are available are comparable. From what is known of the hazards of making such analyses at the present time, it seems exceedingly improbable that such an exercise is reliable for a period in which statistical information and techniques were far less comprehensive than they are now; and, particularly in relation to the 1930s, it is doubtful whether the major economies were sufficiently alike to be compared in this way. The one vital point which such a comparative analysis indirectly emphasises, however, is the dependence of Britain on international, and particularly on European, economic progress as a fundamental condition of its own long-term economic well-being. Until this could be achieved, the future would be clouded.

It may be that, even allowing for the flimsy nature of the statistics, the growth trend of the British economy between 1918 and 1939 was, at best, up to that achieved in the late nineteenth century. But any sensible comparison of growth rates has to involve some attempt to relate what was actually achieved in different periods to what was potentially achievable. It is doubtful whether this can ever be done with any high degree of precision for the two periods under consideration, but the striking feature of the inter-war years, in contrast with the late nineteenth century, was the persistently wide margin of unemployed resources. It is this fact, in association with the available evidence on various aspects of the economy, which justifies a pessimistic view of Britain's economic performance between 1918 and 1939.

Select Bibliography

D. H. Aldcroft, 'Economic Progress in Britain in the 1920s', *Scottish Journal of Political Economy*, xiii (1966). Advances the thesis of 'real economic progress' in the 1920s, based on the 'new' industries. See pp. 19–29 above.

——, 'Economic Growth in Britain in the Inter-War Years: A Reassessment', *Economic History Review*, xx (1967). An optimistic survey of the period based on an eclectic use of statistical data. It contains little new information. See pp. 19–29 above.

——, *British Railways in Transition: The Economic Problems of Britain's Railways since 1914* (1968). A useful survey, though one reviewer has drawn attention to the doubtful accuracy of some of the figures contained therein.

——, *The Inter-War Economy: Britain, 1919–1939* (1970). A generally competent survey, based on secondary sources. However, some of the evidence it presents would seem to conflict with the author's earlier thesis.

——, and P. Fearon (eds), *Economic Growth in Twentieth-Century Britain* (1969). A collection which contains some of the more recent articles on the period, most of which are discussed in detail on pp. 15–29 above.

——, and Harry W. Richardson, *The British Economy, 1870–1939* (1969). Another collection which contains a number of the recent articles on the inter-war years; these are discussed on pp. 15–29 above. A rather lengthy introduction contributes little that is new.

B. W. E. Alford, *W. D. & H. O. Wills and the U.K. Tobacco Industry, 1786–1965* (1972). A comprehensive business history of a major part of a leading consumer-goods industry.

G. C. Allen, *British Industries and their Organisation* (1951 ed.). Contains very informative chapters on each of the major industries of the period. It does not, however, attempt to advance any general interpretation of industrial change.

P. W. S. Andrews and Elizabeth Brunner, *The Life of Lord Nuffield* (1955). Contains interesting analysis and detail on certain aspects of the motor industry in relation to one of its leading entrepreneurs.

W. Ashworth, *An Economic History of England, 1870–1939* (1960). The second part of this book is still by far the best general survey of the period, though it is a little too sparse of statistical information.

——, 'The Late Victorian Economy', *Economica,* xxxiii (1966). Contains a number of interesting observations on long-term factors in British economic growth.

Balfour Committee (Committee on Industry and Trade), *Factors in Industrial and Commercial Efficiency* (part i, 1927; part ii, 1928). Extremely valuable sources of information which contain good introductions to the main items covered in the surveys. These volumes do much to dispel the view that there was a shortage of information available to contemporaries on Britain's economic ills.

Barlow Commission, *Report of the Royal Commission on the Distribution of the Industrial Population,* Cmd 6153 (1940; reprinted 1963). Collects together a lot of data on industrial and urban development during the period. Also indicates the limited nature of the analysis of this important subject.

T. Barna, *The Redistribution of Incomes through Public Finance in 1937* (Oxford, 1945). A somewhat detailed analysis, but it does provide a convenient way of assessing the nature of income distribution and the cumulative effects of social policy at the end of the period.

W. H. Beveridge, *Unemployment: A Problem of Industry* (1930 ed.). Important as a record of the nature of unemployment and as the most important contemporary analysis of the problem. It is a classic work.

A. L. Bowley, *Wages and Income in the United Kingdom since 1860* (1937). This book remains an authoritative study on this apect of economic history. Later studies have to some extent refined Bowley's data but not significantly superseded them.

M. Bowley, 'Some Regional Aspects of the Building Boom, 1924–1936', *Review of Economic Statistics,* v (1937–8). Still the best available account of the boom.

British Association, *Britain in Depression* (1935); *Britain in Recovery* (1938). Twin volumes which contain much useful information, but not much analysis.

A. Bullock, *The Life and Times of Ernest Bevin*, vol 1 (1960). Understandably suffers a little from hero-worship, but by far and away the best book on trade unionism during these years.

D. L. Burn, *The Economic History of Steelmaking, 1867–1939* (1940). A generally sound study of a major staple industry.

N. K. Buxton, 'Economic Progress in the 1920s : A Reappraisal', *Scottish Journal of Political Economy*, XIV (1967); and a following 'Rejoinder' by Aldcroft. A controversy over Aldcroft's interpretation of the available data. It does not add much to the general debate, but at least it illustrates the need to treat statistical information of this kind with extreme care.

——, 'Entrepreneurial Efficiency in the British Coal Industry between the Wars', *Economic History Review*, 2nd ser., XXIII (1970). Emphasises the structural, as opposed to the entrepreneurial, weaknesses of the industry.

A. L. Chapman and R. Knight, *Wages and Salaries in the United Kingdom, 1920–1938* (1953). Contains essential basic data.

Colin Clark, *The Conditions of Economic Progress* (1951 ed.). A valuable source for material on many aspects of economic and social development.

H. Clay, *Lord Norman* (1957). A patient and detailed biography which also contains much on financial history.

D. C. Coleman, *Courtaulds: An Economic and Social History,* vol. 2 : *Rayon* (Oxford, 1969). An excellent business history of the leading firm in a so-called new industry.

W. H. B. Court, 'Problems of the British Coal Industry between the Wars', *Economic History Review*, xv (1945). A most valuable survey.

S. R. Dennison, *The Location of Industry and the Depressed Areas* (1939). A pioneering study in this important field. It contains useful information on industrial development.

J. R. Dowie, 'Growth in the Inter-War Period : Some More Arithmetic', *Economic History Review*, 2nd ser., XXI (1968). A careful working of the available statistical data which does much to undermine the Richardson–Aldcroft–Lomax view of the period.

H. J. Dyos and D. H. Aldcroft, *British Transport: An Economic Survey from the Seventeenth Century to the Twentieth* (1969). The most up-to-date general account. But much more work needs to be done in this field. There are too many books on transport by transport enthusiasts and not enough by economic historians.

C. H. Feinstein, 'Production and Productivity, 1920–1963', *London and Cambridge Economic Bulletin*, XLVIII (1963).

——, 'National Income and Expenditure of the United Kingdom 1870–1963', *London and Cambridge Economic Bulletin*, L (1964). Two major contributions to historical statistics. See pp. 16–29 above.

Bentley B. Gilbert, *British Social Policy*, 1914–1939 (1970). An extremely detailed work by a political historian, but it does contain some interesting general observations, in particular on employment policy.

A. T. K. Grant, *A Study of the Capital Market in Post-War Britain* (1937). Still the best general study available.

K. J. Hancock, 'Unemployment and the Economists in the 1920s', *Economica*, XXVII (1960). An interesting discussion of the shortcomings of contemporary economists in their approach to, and analysis of, unemployment.

——, 'The Reduction of Unemployment as a Problem of Public Policy, 1920–29', *Economic History Review, 2nd ser.*, XV (1962). A very good survey of government policy in this field.

R. F. Harrod, *The Life of John Maynard Keynes* (1951). Essential reading but, when considering the judgements it contains, it is necessary to bear in mind that it is written by an economist and not by an economic historian.

W. G. Hoffmann, *British Industry, 1700–1950* (1955 ed.). This statistical analysis has by no means been superseded by more recent studies. However, it needs to be treated with care. See pp. 16–29 above.

L. J. Hume, 'The Gold Standard and Deflation: Issues and Attitudes in the Nineteen-Twenties', *Economica*, XXX (1963). Demonstrates that Keynes was not the only one to speak out against the financial policy of the twenties.

J. R. Jefferys, *Retail Trading in Britain, 1850–1950* (Cambridge,

1954). An extremely good and, alas, isolated study of a major branch of the service sector.

A. E. Kahn, *Great Britain and the World Economy* (1946). Although to some extent superseded, it is still a very good book on the period. Contains useful statistics on the so-called new industries.

W. T. C. King, *History of the London Discount Market* (1936). Still the best available general account.

H. Leak and A. Maizels, 'The Structure of British Industry', *Journal of the Royal Statistical Society*, cviii (1945). The most useful general statistical analysis of its kind.

W. A. Lewis, *Economic Survey, 1919–1939* (1949). It is doubtful whether many would now agree with the central importance which Lewis attaches to the effects of depression in the international primary-goods sector. But the study still has considerable value as a description of the economic experiences of the major economies.

——, 'World Production, Prices and Trade, 1870–1960', *Manchester School*, xx (1952). Contains useful data. As in the preceding item, this analysis lays considerable emphasis on the importance of the deteriorating position of primary producers.

R. G. Lipsey, 'The Relation between Unemployment and the Rate of Change in Money Wages in the United Kingdom, 1862–1957: A Further Analysis', *Economica*, xxvii (1960). Strong on analysis but a little weak on history. Nevertheless, the hypotheses it advances are useful as starting-points for further study.

K. S. Lomax, 'Production and Productivity Movements in the United Kingdom since 1900', *Journal of the Royal Statistical Society*, series A, cxxii (1959). Useful, but needs to be treated with extreme care. Still a number of major questions hanging over the methods used in this study. See pp. 18–26 above.

——, 'Growth and Productivity in the United Kingdom', *Productivity Measurement Review*, xxxvii (1964). An interpretation of his own production index. See pp 18–26 above.

London and Cambridge Economic Service, *The British Economy: Key Statistics, 1900–1966* (1967). An essential aid to the study of the inter-war years.

Macmillan Committee, *Report of the Committee on Finance and Industry*, Cmd 3897 (1931; reprinted 1961). Essential reading for those professing any specialised interest in the period.

A. Maizels, *Industrial Growth and World Trade* (Cambridge, 1963). An essential reference book. At the same time, however, it illustrates how much more work needs to be done in this field.

R. C. O. Matthews, 'Some Aspects of Post-War Growth in the British Economy in Relation to Historical Experience', *Transactions of the Manchester Statistical Society* (1964). A very clear exposition of the main trends in the economy.

G. Maxcy and A. Silberston, *The Motor Industry* (1959). Contains useful information on the development of the industry over the inter-war years. The definitive history of this important industry is, however, yet to be written.

May Committee, *Committee on National Expenditure*, Cmd 3920 (1931). One of the most influential and misguided official reports in recent economic history. For this reason alone it is essential reading.

Alan S. Milward, *The Economic Effects of the Two World Wars on Britain* (1970). A companion volume in the series of which this book is a part.

B. R. Mitchell and Phyllis Deane, *Abstract of British Historical Statistics* (Cambridge, 1962). A mine of information, though the series it contains are necessarily of uneven quality.

D. E. Moggridge, *The Return to Gold, 1925: The Formulation of Economic Policy and its Critics* (Cambridge, 1969). An interesting description of the individuals involved in and events surrounding this episode, but the economic arguments it advances are questionable. See pp. 30–9 above.

C. L Mowat, *Britain between the Wars, 1918–1940* (1955). An excellent general survey of the political, social and economic history of these years; though, not surprisingly, in some instances it has been superseded.

E. Nevin, 'The Origins of Cheap Money: 1931–1932', *Economica,* xx (1953). A clear and useful analysis.

——, *The Mechanism of Cheap Money: A Study of British Monetary Policy, 1931–1939* (1955). A comprehensive and balanced account.

A. T. Peacock and J. Wiseman, *The Growth of Public Expenditure in the United Kingdom* (1967 ed.). This has become the standard work on the subject.

E. H. Phelps Brown with Margaret Browne, *A Century of Pay* (1968). Despite the obvious limitations to a statistical exercise of this kind, it is an impressive study. Moreover, although primarily statistical in character, it shows sound historical sense.

——, and B. Weber, 'Accumulation, Productivity and Distribution in the British Economy, 1870–1938', *Economic Journal*, LXIII (1953). One of the earliest studies in this field, but it still contains some useful data.

A. W. Phillips, 'The Relation between Unemployment and the Rate of Change of Money Wages in the United Kingdom, 1861–1959', *Economica*, XXV (1958). An interesting analysis but not critical enough of the nature of the historical evidence it uses.

Political and Economic Planning (P.E.P.), *The Market for Household Appliances* (1945). Particularly useful in showing how limited were sales of these goods at the end of the inter-war years.

S. Pollard, *The Development of the British Economy, 1914–1967* (1969). A comprehensive survey, but the amount of detail it contains tends to obscure some shrewd analytical insights.

——, *The Gold Standard and Employment Policies between the Wars* (1970). A collection of articles on this theme. The editor's introduction is too narrow in its approach. Lays heavy stress on the importance of monetary policy. See pp. 30–9 above.

M. M. Postan, *British War Production* (1952). The early chapters are particularly revealing on the economic effects of the rearmament programme and on the shortcomings which existed in important sectors of British industry at the end of the thirties.

H. W. Richardson, 'The New Industries between the Wars', *Oxford Economic Papers*, XIII (1961). An interesting attempt to argue the case for the importance of the 'new' industries in the 1930s. In view of subsequent analysis, however, the thesis would seem to be considerably overstated. See pp. 15–26 above.

——, 'The Basis of Economic Recovery in the 1930s : A Review and a New Interpretation', *Economic History Review*, 2nd ser., xv (1962). A somewhat eclectic attempt to argue the case for 'recovery' in the 1930s. Unfortunately, the author does not sufficiently define what he means by 'recovery'; and indeed, much of the argument advanced here is undermined by Dowie (1968). See pp. 15–26 above.

——, 'Over-commitment in Britain before 1930', *Oxford Economic Papers*, xvii (1965). A very general statement of a very complex problem. A great deal more research needs to be done before one can generalise on this subject.

——, *Economic Recovery in Britain, 1932–9* (1967). A useful study which contains much of interest. Unfortunately, the author has an overriding determination to prove his thesis. Although the work suffers from the same weaknesses as the article on the subject cited above, by comparison the conclusions it draws are somewhat modified.

S. B. Saul, 'The American Impact on British Industry, 1895–1914', *Business History*, iii (1960). A warning against the view that British industry was significantly backward even before the First World War. A corrective to the 'over-commitment' thesis.

——, 'The Motor Industry in Britain to 1914', *Business History*, v (1962). Essential to an understanding of the subsequent development of the industry.

R. S. Sayers, 'The Springs of Technical Progress in Britain, 1919–39', *Economic Journal*, lx (1950). A convenient catalogue of major technical changes. However, the author's evaluation of these changes would seem to overstate their general economic impact.

——, 'The Return to Gold, 1925', chap. xii in L. S. Pressnell (ed.), *Studies in the Industrial Revolution* (1960). Like Moggridge (1969), Sayers deals with the events surrounding this episode. His most important argument, however, is that which questions whether monetary policy was of primary importance. See p. 30–9 above.

——, *A History of Economic Change in England, 1880–1939* (Oxford, 1967). A generally straightforward, brief introductory account, though the manner in which it deals with 'old' and 'new' industries is not altogether satisfactory.

S. G. Sturmey, *The Economic Development of Radio* (1958). A useful account, but it illustrates the need for more detailed business histories in this field.

——, *British Shipping and World Competition* (1962). A very good analysis of this important industry.

I. Svennilson, *Growth and Stagnation in the European Economy* (Geneva, 1954). A masterly study of Western Europe, including the U.K., in the inter-war period. A mine of information and analysis on all aspects of economic development.

H. Tyszynski, 'World Trade in Manufactured Commodities, 1899–1950', *Manchester School,* xix (1951). A very valuable study which, among other things, analyses some of the reasons behind Britain's declining trading position.

G. Walker, *Road and Rail* (1947 ed.). A comprehensive account of transport policy. Emphasises the lack of official understanding of the relationship between road and rail transport.

D. Williams, 'Montagu Norman and Banking Policy in the 1920s', *Yorkshire Bulletin of Economic and Social Research,* xi (1959). A good account of monetary policy, though perhaps a little too kind to the authorities in general and to Norman in particular. Makes the important point that monetary policy was not an underlying cause of unemployment.

——, 'London and the 1931 Financial Crisis', *Economic History Review,* 2nd ser., xv (1962–3). An analysis of the weaknesses of the gold exchange standard which operated from 1925 until its demise in 1931, as compared with the strengths of the pre-war system.

——, 'The 1931 Financial Crisis', *Yorkshire Bulletin of Economic and Social Research,* xv (1963). A detailed treatment of the crisis in international terms.

C. Wilson, *The History of Unilever* (1954). A good business history of this important firm. The approach to the subject, however, is that of the historian rather than of the economic historian, and some important questions are therefore not considered.

D. Winch, *Economics and Policy: An Historical Study* (1969). A very useful study which deals mainly with the inter-war years. A little overawed by Keynes, but this is perhaps excusable in an economist. Suffers a little by concentrating too much on the internal battles between academic economists at the expense of a fuller discussion of the relationship between economic thought and policy. Nevertheless it is a pioneering effort in an important field.

A. J. Youngson, *Britain's Economic Growth, 1920–1966* (1967). A book of uneven quality, since the author is prepared to base much of his analysis of the period between the wars on *The Economist*, which suffered from a number of misconceptions during those years. Nevertheless the chapter dealing with economic thought and economic policy is a very useful brief survey.

Index

95

precision instruments industry, 20
prices: German, 35; international, 33, 35; U.S.A., 31; of 'new' products, 23, 45
Priestley, J. B., 13
primary product prices, 22
productivity, 16, 20–1, 25, 47
professional services, 76
public corporations, 71
public works, 70

railways, 70–1
rayon industry, 21, 45, 47, 48, 51, 61
rearmament, 46–7, 55, 61, 75
'recovery' in the 1930s, 16–19, 20–1, 50, 61–2, 77, 81–2
regional unemployment, 74–5
reparations, 33, 63
'residual', 42
return to the gold standard, 30–9
Richardson, H. W., 16, 17, 21, 51, 75, 77, 89, 90
road transport, 70–1
Robbins, L., 73
Robertson, D. H., 69
rubber industry, 45, 52

Saul, S. B., 48, 80, 90
Sayers, R. S., 15, 32, 34, 51, 90
service and distribution industry, 20, 28, 56
shipbuilding industry, 46–7, 52, 75, 76
shipping industry, 52, 53, 62
Shirras, G. F., and Rostas, L., 78 n.
silk industry, 21, 47
Snowden, P., 67
social overhead capital, 49–50
social services, 78
Special Areas, 69
standardisation of goods, 52
staple industries, 19, 22–3, 34, 46–7, 50, 56, 61, 79
statistical information, quality and availability of, 22–8, 71
structural change, 17, 30, 37, 41–2, 47–8, 49–50, 52–3, 56, 68–70, 77
Sturmey, S. G., 52, 90

sub-contracting, 24
Supple, B., 28 n.
Svennilson, I., 15, 91

tariffs, 18, 60–1
taxation, 78
technical education, 53
technical innovation, 16, 18, 19, 21, 40–1, 43, 45–6, 50–2, 53–4, 55
terms of trade, 18, 27–8, 58
textiles, 21, 24, 46–7, 76
tobacco industry, 51, 53
trade, 55–6, 57–62; see also exports, imports
trade and growth, 62
trade cycle, autonomous theory of, 17
trade groups, international, 58–9, 61–2
trade unions, 76–7, 78–9
tramway and omnibus services, 75
transport and communications, 76
transport policy, 70–1
Treasury, 30, 31, 32, 65, 68, 71, 73
T.U.C., 79
Tyszynski, H., 91

unemployment, 17, 22, 25, 29, 30, 46, 48, 49, 56, 67–8, 69, 70, 74–5, 77, 79, 82
Unemployment Assistance Board (1934), 68
Unilever, 53
unit wage costs, 35
utility industries, 20, 76

wages, 75–8; see also unit wage costs
Walker, G., 91
weighting problems in production indices, 22–8
Wicksell Lectures, 59 n.
Williams, B. R., 36 n.
Williams, D., 34, 91
Wilson, C., 53, 91
Winch, D., 68, 72, 91
woollen industry, 46, 59; see also textiles

Youngson, A. J., 32, 69 n., 92